CAREC HEALTH STRATEGY 2030

MAY 2022

CONTENTS

TABLES, FIGURES, AND BOXES

TABLES

FIGURES

BOXES

ABBREVIATIONS

ABEC	–	Almaty–Bishkek Economic Corridor
ADB	–	Asian Development Bank
CAREC	–	Central Asia Regional Economic Cooperation
CDC	–	Center for Disease Control (USA)
COVID-19	–	coronavirus disease
CVD	–	cardiovascular disease
EOC	–	emergency operating center (for pandemic management)
FCTC	–	Framework Convention on Tobacco Control (WHO)
FETP	–	Field Epidemiology Training Program
GDP	–	gross domestic product
ICT	–	information and communication technology
ICU	–	intensive care unit
IHR	–	International Health Regulations
IPC	–	infection prevention and control
IT	–	information technology
LQMS	–	laboratory quality management system
MDR-TB	–	multidrug-resistant tuberculosis
NCD	–	noncommunicable disease
OECD	–	Organisation for Economic Co-operation and Development
PCR	–	polymerase chain reaction
PHC	–	primary health care
PIP PC	–	Pandemic Influenza Preparedness Framework Partnership Contribution
PPE	–	personal protective equipment
PRC	–	People's Republic of China
QMS	–	quality management system
RCCE	–	risk communication and community engagement
RHC	–	regional health cooperation
SARS	–	severe acute respiratory syndrome
SDG	–	Sustainable Development Goals
SOM	–	Senior Officials' Meeting
SOP	–	standard operating procedure
SPECA	–	Special Programme for the Economies of Central Asia (UN)
TEPHINET	–	Training Programs in Epidemiology and Public Health Interventions Network
UN	–	United Nations
UNICEF	–	United Nations Children's Fund
UHC	–	universal health coverage
WGH	–	Working Group on Health
WHO	–	World Health Organization

EXECUTIVE SUMMARY

The Central Asia Regional Economic Cooperation (CAREC) 2030 Strategy focuses on five operational clusters, including human development with a new operational cluster on health cooperation. This cluster aims to improve health system performance in responding to public health threats and enhance regional health security. The coronavirus disease (COVID-19) pandemic has highlighted the importance of health security. As public health threats such as infectious disease outbreaks can quickly become a cross-border concern, regional health cooperation is key to achieving health security among CAREC countries.

The CAREC Health Strategy 2030 supports health cooperation under the human development cluster of CAREC 2030, with focus on enhancing health security through regional cooperation. It aligns with other CAREC strategies such as CAREC Gender Strategy 2030, which lays out entry points for gender mainstreaming for the human development pillar under CAREC 2030. The beneficiaries of this strategy include the population (including migrants and vulnerable population groups), ministries of health of CAREC countries and those managing and working in the health system, and development partners active in the region.

The vision of the CAREC Health Strategy 2030 is—"public health threats in the CAREC region are addressed comprehensively, efficiently and sustainably, through adopting a regional approach, while safeguarding the needs of the most vulnerable segments of the population." Its guiding principles include cooperation among countries, multisector coordination, a focus on benefiting the population, ensuring feasibility combined with an evidence-based approach, safeguarding sustainability and ownership, and alignment with international policies and frameworks.

The CAREC Health Strategy 2030 builds on four main pillars: (i) leadership and human resource capacity, (ii) technical preparedness (laboratories and surveillance), (iii) surge demands and access to supplies, and (iv) vulnerable population groups and border health. Implementation of the pillars is enabled by the CAREC-supported institutional setup including the Working Group on Health (WGH); cooperation and partnerships based on stakeholder engagement with political commitment and policy dialogue, multisector coordination, and geographic clusters; and capacity support through training, research, and knowledge sharing.

Pillar 1 aims to strengthen regional leadership, coordination, and workforce capacity. To better respond to epidemic and pandemic health threats, improvements in interministerial and multisector policy coordination and international support and health system governance capacity in the CAREC region are planned. Sufficient workforce skills and capacity are required, especially in public health emergency leadership, public health, epidemiology, and research. This should result in effective planning and implementation of measures and innovations in response to public health threats, including the COVID-19 pandemic.

Pillar 2 will support the improvement of surveillance and laboratory infrastructure. This will be carried out by ensuring an effective surveillance response to public health threats, including the COVID-19 pandemic. This may include improving surveillance systems, exploring regional dashboards with automated early-warning systems, and establishing regionally aligned awareness-raising materials on communicable diseases.

Sufficient laboratory infrastructure and management according to international quality and biosafety requirements will be needed.

Pillar 3 intends to increase capacity to meet surge demands and access to supplies with a focus on three main aspects: (i) ensure effective and harmonized regulatory mechanisms and standards for medications and supplies, (ii) develop efficient national and regional procurement mechanisms for medications and supplies, and (iii) strengthen the reliability of supply chain management that assures sufficient supply and stocks for emergency situations in the region.

Pillar 4 will enhance health services for migrants, border communities, and vulnerable groups. Access to health services and cross-border referrals will be improved. Efforts will be needed to decrease the burden of communicable diseases among migrants, border communities, and vulnerable population groups. Effective infection prevention and control measures, including for COVID-19 cases, will be supported in border regions to protect travelers and the population.

Crosscutting issues across all four pillars include digital health with innovations to support health information systems; data management; regional knowledge sharing; and improved capacity to develop, implement, and utilize innovative digital technologies and solutions. Disaggregation of data by gender will be fostered and specific needs of women considered in health planning and design of services and infrastructure.

Implementation of the CAREC Health Strategy 2030 will be supported through the existing CAREC institutional structure. Strategy implementation will be led by the CAREC WGH. This group is composed of high-level representatives from health-related government agencies who were appointed by each CAREC country since March 2021. The WGH will be complemented with multidisciplinary expertise in various sectors on a need basis. The WGH would also involve development partner representatives, including World Health Organization (WHO) representatives as observers, upon their willingness and availability. The CAREC Secretariat is responsible for providing technical, administrative, and organizational support during implementation of the strategy. There will be regular reporting of implementation progress against the work plan. Results will guide forward planning and milestone review and provide lessons for adjusting activities and implementation mechanisms.

A regional investment framework on health will be developed to translate the strategic directions of the CAREC Health Strategy 2030 and overall CAREC 2030 into a medium-term pipeline of regional projects and initiatives under the four strategic pillars to be implemented during the first 5 years of the strategy implementation period (2022–2026). The framework will be developed to help guide partner investments and meet the gap in effectively addressing key regional needs, including protecting vulnerable populations in border areas.

This strategy is the result of extensive consultations with CAREC WGH members; country technical experts; government stakeholders; and development partners, including WHO. It is based on a situational analysis including national assessments and is intended as a tool to guide CAREC health programming and mobilize new project financing.

1

INTRODUCTION

1. The Central Asia Regional Economic Cooperation (CAREC) Program is a partnership of 11 countries (Afghanistan, Azerbaijan, the People's Republic of China [PRC], Georgia, Kazakhstan, the Kyrgyz Republic, Mongolia, Pakistan, Tajikistan, Turkmenistan, and Uzbekistan) and development partners working together to promote development through cooperation, leading to accelerated economic growth and shared prosperity. CAREC operations are guided by the CAREC 2030 Strategy endorsed at the 16th CAREC Ministerial Conference in October 2017. The CAREC 2030 Strategy focuses on five operational clusters, including human development, a new operational cluster, to better address the region's development needs and help its member countries achieve the 2030 Global Development Agenda. CAREC 2030 supports CAREC countries in addressing pandemic risks and control of communicable and noncommunicable diseases (NCDs). The coronavirus disease (COVID-19) pandemic has highlighted the importance of health security.[1] As public health threats such as infectious disease outbreaks can quickly cross borders and become a cross-border concern, regional health cooperation is key to achieving health security among CAREC countries.

2. As an initial step to explore opportunities for promoting regional cooperation in the health sector, a scoping study was carried out by the Asian Development Bank (ADB) in 2019 and 2020.[2] The study reviewed CAREC health sector challenges and progress, and recommended establishing a regional health coordination mechanism and developing a regional health strategy and investment framework. It also recommended regional cooperation in three areas, namely (i) regional health security; (ii) health systems strengthening through regional cooperation; and (iii) improving health services for migrants, mobile populations, and border communities. The scoping study was presented and discussed with CAREC governments and development partners on 15 October 2020 and published in July 2021. A CAREC Working Group on Health (WGH) was established in March 2021 to guide CAREC health cooperation and the development of a CAREC health strategy toward 2030. The development of the strategy involved inputs from the CAREC countries and development partners like the World Health Organization (WHO) and the World Bank.[3]

3. The CAREC Health Strategy 2030 elaborates areas of cooperation focusing on enhancing health security through regional cooperation. It aligns with other CAREC strategies such as CAREC Gender Strategy 2030, which lays out entry points for gender mainstreaming for the human development pillar under CAREC 2030.[4] The beneficiaries of this strategy include the population (including migrants and the vulnerable population groups), ministries of health of CAREC countries and those managing and working in the health system, and development partners active in the region. Under the CAREC Health Strategy, regional health cooperation will have a strong foundation to build on for the future.[5]

---

[1] World Health Organization (WHO) defines global public health security as "the activities required, both proactive and reactive, to minimize the danger and impact of acute public health events that endanger people's health across geographical regions and international boundaries." See World Health Organization. Health Security. https://www.who.int/health-topics/health-security#tab=tab_1.

[2] ADB. 2021. *Toward CAREC 2030: Enhancing Regional Cooperation in the Health Sector—A Scoping Study*. Manila.

[3] A consortium, led by GOPA Worldwide Consultants, was selected to manage a multidisciplinary team of international and national experts to provide capacity development, analysis, and implementation support. The objectives are to prepare, mitigate, and respond to regional health threats, including the current COVID-19 outbreak, and support the preparation of the *CAREC Health Strategy 2030* and *Regional Investment Framework*.

[4] ADB. 2021. *CAREC Gender Strategy 2030: Inclusion, Empowerment, and Resilience for All*. Manila.

[5] This strategy was prepared based on the information available as of 31 July 2021.

2

IMPORTANCE OF REGIONAL HEALTH COOPERATION

4.   One of the most important lessons that pandemics teach the world is that—"together, we are stronger." An outbreak such as the COVID-19 pandemic has reemphasized that global and regional cooperation is needed to overcome health threats.[6] It has amplified the importance of better-controlled pandemic situations through strengthening regional cooperation for health. Local control measures alone can slow down but not stop outbreaks. Alongside collaboration with global institutions, regional cooperation may offer significant benefits to many low- and middle-income countries, ranging from informal cooperation, setting up joint projects (e.g., building common infrastructure), coordinating policies and regulatory frameworks to shaping joint policies and institutions.[7] Achieving regional health security is a crucial entry point for regional health cooperation (RHC) of CAREC countries.

5.   The concept of international cooperation for surveillance and to counter emerging and high-risk infectious diseases was already minted with the creation of WHO International Health Regulations (IHR) in 1969, later revised in 2005 in the wake of the severe acute respiratory syndrome (SARS) epidemic. WHO member countries endorsed the updated IHR principles in 2005, after which global agreement was to start implementing this collaborative framework by 2007. As defined and signed off by WHO partner countries, participating countries agreed to share surveillance data and alert WHO and partner countries on events seen as high-risk outbreaks. Several events have since been reported, and countermeasures for control of threatening pandemics have been coordinated by WHO in partnership with participating countries and regional and international organizations.

6.   Since the 2009 H1N1 influenza pandemic, several high-level panels and commissions have made specific recommendations to improve global pandemic preparedness, including the implementation of the IHR (2005). However, most recommendations were never implemented. National pandemic preparedness has been vastly underfunded, despite the clear evidence that its cost is a fraction of the cost of responses and losses incurred when an epidemic occurs. Owing to these gaps, the Independent Panel for Pandemic Preparedness and Response recommends maintaining political commitment to pandemic preparedness between emergencies and to response during emergencies, as well as ensuring maximum complementarity, cooperation, and collective action.[8]

7.   RHC is key in managing health security risks and supporting national health systems' resilience to better respond to public health threats like the current COVID-19 pandemic. It provides an opportunity for change, particularly since the importance of health interdependency between countries is becoming increasingly recognized.[9] The need for regional cooperation is also supported by WHO Regional Office for Europe, European Programme of Work 2020–2025, which lays out the vision of member states of WHO European Region. It emphasizes the need for cooperation and solidarity and the need to mobilize regional and subregional structures.[10]

[6]   Organization of American States. n.d. *Alliance for Multilateralism: We Need Strong Global Cooperation and Solidarity to Fight COVID-19.* https://www.oas.org/fpdb/press/Declaration-AfM-COVID-final.pdf.

[7]   A.B. Amaya and P. De Lombaerde. 2021. Regional Cooperation is Essential to Combatting Health Emergencies in the Global South. *Globalization and Health.* 17(9).

[8]   In May 2020, the World Health Assembly requested the director-general of WHO to initiate an impartial, independent, and comprehensive review of the international health response to COVID-19 and of experiences gained and lessons learned from that, and to make recommendations for improving future capacities. The director-general asked H.E. Ellen Johnson Sirleaf and the Rt Hon. Helen Clark to convene an independent panel for this purpose and to report to the World Health Assembly in May 2021.

[9]   I. Kickbusch, G. Silberschmidt, and P. Buss. 2007. Global Health Diplomacy: The Need for New Perspectives, Strategic Approaches and Skills in Global Health. *Bulletin World Health Organization.* 85(3). pp. 230–232.

[10]   World Health Organization. 2021. *European Programme of Work, 2020–2025.* Geneva.

3

HEALTH SECURITY
IN CAREC

A. Threats to Health Security in the Region

8. The CAREC region is especially prone to outbreaks and epidemics due to its increasing connectivity, population mobility, urban hubs, and livestock raising and trading. Located at the crossroads of global value chains, countries in the CAREC region rely heavily on labor migration, as well as livestock production, which is an important contributor to the economies of most CAREC countries and a significant part of cross-border trade. Hence, the region is particularly vulnerable to zoonotic diseases outbreaks that may continue to occur in the future (footnote 2). There is a persistent threat from emerging infectious diseases such as COVID-19, pandemic influenza, and other viruses with pandemic potential that can move across continents within a few months. Most of the emerging infectious diseases and endemic infectious diseases are of zoonotic origin.

9. Some CAREC countries are also exposed to outbreaks of other communicable diseases such as malaria, dengue, and Japanese encephalitis that may spread regionally. Chronic infectious diseases, such as HIV/AIDS, tuberculosis (TB), and viral hepatitis B and C, continue to be a heavy burden in the region. Viral hepatitis B and C are highly prevalent in all CAREC countries. The PRC (14%) and Pakistan (10%) account for almost a quarter of the hepatitis C (HCV) burden among the 28 countries, accounting for 80% of the HCV burden globally.[11] The incidence of TB, although declining across the CAREC region, continues to pose a major threat even in its uncomplicated form and especially in the form of multidrug-resistant TB (MDR-TB).[12]

10. Antimicrobial resistance constitutes a significant regional health concern. Resistance to inexpensive and effective antimicrobial drugs has emerged at an alarmingly high rate, making many common diseases and pathogens (such as TB) difficult and expensive to treat. Nosocomial (hospital-acquired) infections pose an increasing public health threat with global dimensions and are associated with poor hospital infection prevention and control (IPC), poor or inexistent quality assurance, antimicrobial resistance, and low private sector interest in developing new medicines with limited market potential.[13]

B. Impact of Health Security Threats in the Region

11. Public health threats such as infectious disease outbreaks can cause devastating effects on human lives and economies, and add a significant burden to health systems.

12. **Impact on human lives.** The COVID-19 pandemic has demonstrated the catastrophic impact public health threats can have on human lives. For many households in the region, COVID-19 is posing difficulties due to a combination of three factors: (i) the loss of income from informal work, (ii) the loss of remittances as migrant workers are no longer able to work, and (iii) price inflation from lower trade and increase in the price of agriculture commodities.[14] The loss of income from informal work is a large issue for

---

[11]   World Health Organization. 2017. *Global Hepatitis Report*. Geneva.

[12]   The average TB incidence rate in the WHO/Europe region declined from 5.4% in 2006–2015 to 3.3% in 2014–2015.

[13]   Zhussupova et al. 2021. Evaluation of Antibiotic Use in Kazakhstan for the Period 2017–2019 Based on WHO Access, Watch and Reserve Classification (AWaRe 2019). *Antibiotics*. 10 (1). p. 58; ADB. 2021. *Toward CAREC 2030: Enhancing Regional Cooperation in the Health Sector—A Scoping Study*. Manila; Food and Agriculture Organization of the United Nations. 2019. *Mongolia at the Crossroads for Antibiotic Resistance*. Rome; C.S. Marchello, S.D. Carr, and J.A. Crump. 2020. A Systematic Review on Antimicrobial Resistance among Salmonella Typhi Worldwide. *Am J Trop Med Hyg*. 103 (6). pp. 2518–2527; D.J. Ulmasova et al. 2013. Multidrug-Resistant Tuberculosis in Uzbekistan: Results of a Nationwide Survey, 2010 to 2011. *Euro Surveill*. 18 (42).

[14]   United Nations Development Programme (UNDP). 2020. *COVID-19 and Central Asia: Socioeconomic Impacts and Key Policy Considerations for Recovery*. New York.

CAREC countries. Around 45% of Georgia's labor force is employed outside the formal sector, 25% for Kazakhstan, 39% for Tajikistan, and 70% for the Kyrgyz Republic.[15] Many individuals who work in the informal sector lost their jobs due to the restrictions imposed throughout the pandemic period. Further, the high proportion of migrant labor shows a decline in remittances (footnote 14). The World Bank estimated a 28% decrease in remittances to Central Asia in 2020.[16] The loss of income and insufficient social protection has resulted in households of migrant and informal workers being at risk of falling into poverty. In addition, price inflation, specifically of food, resulted in a large percentage of the population facing food and nutrition insecurity (footnote 14). About 58% of the estimated 2.4 million individuals who will be pushed into poverty in Europe and Central Asia live in Central Asia.[17] All these factors have deepened already existing inequalities, including between men and women.[18] Among the gender inequalities are gaps in labor force participation across the region, as well as disparities in employment rates, pay scales, and quality of employment. Women are also facing greater difficulties in accessing healthcare since their pressure to undertake primary care responsibilities is much higher than that of men (footnote 4).

13. During lockdowns, the low quality of housing in many countries, including in some CAREC countries, has also harshly affected mental health. The overall burden on women caused by the COVID-19 pandemic especially affected their mental and emotional health. An assessment done in Europe and Central Asia by the United Nations (UN) Women revealed that women's psychological and mental health is being affected at higher rates than that of men.[19]

14. **Impact on economy.**[20] Before the COVID-19 outbreak, other public health threats had demonstrated their adverse impact on the economy. SARS, which only resulted in approximately 8,000 people getting infected and a case fatality rate of about 10%, resulted in a loss of at least $40 billion and a gross domestic product (GDP) slowdown of 1%.[21] The COVID-19 pandemic has adversely impacted the economies in the CAREC region. A combination of factors caused economic vulnerability, including increased reliance on commodities. The impact of quarantines and lockdowns has affected wholesale and retail trade, decimated the tourism sector, raised food prices, led to loss of employment and rise in poverty, and lowered access to finance for small and medium enterprises. Despite a clear adverse impact on economies in 2020, there is evidence that the average CAREC region real GDP growth turned positive in the first quarter of 2021 after negative growth rates throughout 2020 (footnote 16). In the first quarter of 2021, real GDP grew by 2.9% on average in the CAREC region, and further acceleration is forecast for the rest of the year and 2022. These projections depend, first and foremost, on how quickly countries can vaccinate their populations and how much global recovery poses a benefit to them (footnote 16).

[15] Economic and Social Commission for Asia and the Pacific (UNESCAP). 2021. *COVID-19 in North and Central Asia: Impacts, Responses and Strategies to Build Back Better.* Bangkok.

[16] CAREC Institute. 2021. *Quarterly Economic Monitor.* No. 3. Urumqi.

[17] Organisation for Economic Co-operation and Development (OECD). 2020. *COVID-19 Crisis Response in Central Asia.* Paris.

[18] T. Khitarishvili. 2016. Gender Dimensions of Inequality in the Countries of Central Asia, South Caucasus, and Western CIS. *Working Paper Series.* No. 858. New York: Levy Economics Institute of Bard College; United Nations Children's Fund (UNICEF). 2016. *Rapid Review on Inclusion and Gender Equality in Central and Eastern Europe, the Caucasus and Central Asia.* Geneva; OECD. 2019. *Draft Background Note Promoting Gender Equality in Eurasia: Better Policies for Women's Economic Empowerment.* Paris.

[19] UN Women. 2020. *The Impact of COVID-19 on Women's and Men's Lives and Livelihoods in Europe and Central Asia: Preliminary Results from a Rapid Gender Assessment.* Istanbul.

[20] The analysis mainly focuses on health and human impacts, while economic impact is only summarized briefly.

[21] Institute of Medicine (US) Forum on Microbial Threats. 2004. *Learning from SARS: Preparing for the Next Disease Outbreak: Workshop Summary.* Washington, DC.

15. **Impact on health systems.** The long-term impact of the COVID-19 crisis on the health systems of CAREC countries is still unclear. As of September 2021, COVID-19 had caused more than 4.1 million infections and 75,000 deaths in the CAREC region (Table 1). Many health systems could not cope with the sudden influx of patients (footnote 14). There were a multitude of insufficiencies, including, but not limited to, poor primary care capacity; lack of hospital beds; lack of healthcare workers; poor disease surveillance capacity; and lack of personal protective equipment (PPE), ventilators, and medications.[22] While evidence on the impact on population health outcomes is still emerging, many countries struggled to maintain essential health services and routine immunizations while coping with COVID-19. These short-term impacts show areas that need strengthening in the future and present many lessons learned. At the same time, considerable investments in health systems have been made following the COVID-19 outbreak, which need to be leveraged strategically to build resilient health systems. These investments are an opportunity to improve health security across the region.

C. Drivers of Health Security in the Region

16. A number of factors shape regional health security, including health systems capacity, climate change, migration, and sustainable financing. Responding to health security threats requires capacity for risk reduction (prevention, preparedness, and mitigation) and health systems' resilience building at local, national, regional, and global levels (Figure 1).

Table 1: COVID-19 Cases and Deaths in CAREC Countries

Country	Total Cases (Confirmed)	Cases per Million	Total Deaths	Deaths per Million
Afghanistan	147,154	3,694	6,708	168
Azerbaijan	343,849	33,634	5,023	491
China, People's Republic of	93,066	64	4,636	3
Georgia	419,534	105,417	5,820	1,462
Kazakhstan	633,469	33,349	9,077	478
Kyrgyz Republic	162,892	24,575	2,325	351
Mongolia	164,155	49,306	815	245
Pakistan	1,034,837	4,595	23,422	104
Tajikistan	15,482	1,588	122	13
Turkmenistan	NA	NA	NA	NA
Uzbekistan	129,327	3,811	874	26

Source: Our World in Data. Statistics and Research: Coronavirus Pandemic (COVID-19). https://ourworldindata.org/coronavirus (accessed 31 July 2021). Data for Turkmenistan are not available.

---

[22] V.S. Balakrishnan. 2020. COVID-19 Response in Central Asia. *The Lancet Microbe.* 1 (7). p. e281.

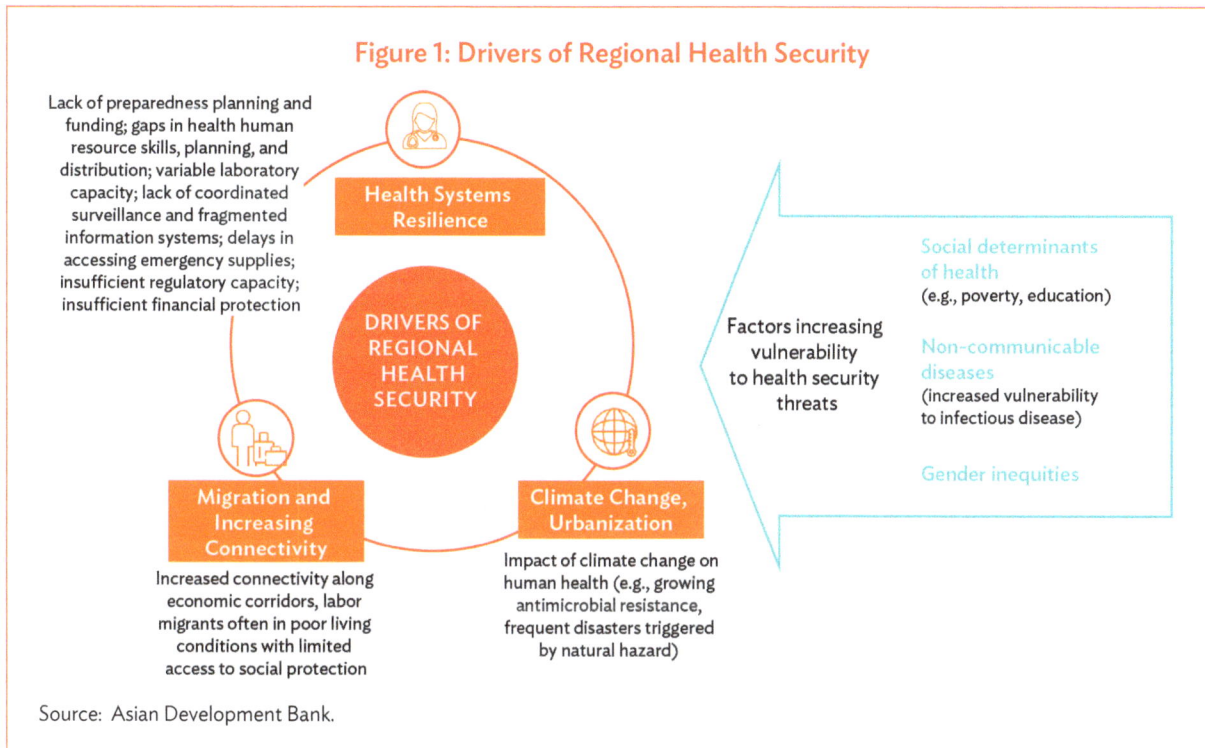

Figure 1: Drivers of Regional Health Security

Lack of preparedness planning and funding; gaps in health human resource skills, planning, and distribution; variable laboratory capacity; lack of coordinated surveillance and fragmented information systems; delays in accessing emergency supplies; insufficient regulatory capacity; insufficient financial protection

Health Systems Resilience

DRIVERS OF REGIONAL HEALTH SECURITY

Migration and Increasing Connectivity

Climate Change, Urbanization

Increased connectivity along economic corridors, labor migrants often in poor living conditions with limited access to social protection

Impact of climate change on human health (e.g., growing antimicrobial resistance, frequent disasters triggered by natural hazard)

Factors increasing vulnerability to health security threats

Social determinants of health (e.g., poverty, education)

Non-communicable diseases (increased vulnerability to infectious disease)

Gender inequities

Source: Asian Development Bank.

17. **Governance.** Countries that have been hit by past pandemics, like H1N1, have proven to have better pandemic plans in place for COVID-19 and to act promptly (footnote 21). Such countries had well-functioning and clear governance structures and mechanisms for effective national response, including multisector collaboration, whole-of-government approaches, and involvement of the private sector and civil society organizations.[23]

18. The experience from the 2003 SARS outbreak underlined the importance of early detection, effective communication to the public,

the promotion of research and development, strategies for containment, and international collaboration in implementing such strategies (footnote 21). Similarly, the lessons from the H1N1 2009–2010 pandemic highlighted the importance of different strategies, including accelerating the implementation of the core capacities required by the IHR, creating a contingency fund for public health emergencies, and establishing a more extensive public health reserve workforce.[24] In the Kyrgyz Republic, Tajikistan, Turkmenistan, and Uzbekistan, the Pandemic Influenza Preparedness Framework Partnership Contribution (PIP PC),

---

[23] In Mongolia, for instance, all decisions for action were launched with clear allocation of responsibilities to key authorities such as the Ministry of Health, the State Emergency Commission, and the National Center for Infectious Diseases (also the national hub for disease surveillance).

[24] H.V. Fineberg. 2014. Pandemic Preparedness and Response: Lessons from the H1N1 Influenza of 2009. *N Engl J Med.* 370 (14). pp. 1335–1342. The cases of Mongolia and the PRC show that an effective COVID-19 containment may in part be due to preparedness and experience from previous high-risk infections such as plague, cholera, and other SARS viruses. Due to recurrent outbreaks, the Mongolian health system already had routines in place and experience to draw from. The health system and government officials have learned how to collaborate well to track, isolate, and treat those who are infected and to achieve successful disease control and containment.

established with WHO support in 2014, proved to be useful for greater preparedness for the influenza pandemic.[25]

19. A review of the state of pandemic preparedness before COVID-19 showed that national pandemic preparedness has been vastly underfunded in many countries, despite the clear evidence that it costs a fraction of the cost of responses and losses incurred when an epidemic occurs (footnote 24). (An overview of lessons learned from COVID-19 can be found in Appendix 5). Although the IHR and various regional frameworks are in place to support countries in improving health security and addressing threats, competing priorities for national budgets made implementation difficult and led to limited health system investment required to protect health security.[26] Globally, the COVID-19 pandemic revealed that response funding was not released rapidly enough and in a structured manner to take quick action.[27] Based on the results of national assessments, despite budgetary limitations, many CAREC countries have been able to mobilize additional budgetary resources to take an immediate spending action for COVID-19 response (i.e., to support health and other essential services during the pandemic). Some examples are provided in Box 1.

Box 1: Mobilizing Additional Budget Resources to Fight COVID-19 in CAREC Countries

(i) As part of immediate spending action, the government stimulus package was introduced in Pakistan, and these funds have been utilized, such as for the procurement of urgent supplies and strengthening of hospital services. In addition, an Asian Development Bank loan was granted to Pakistan for the COVID-19 Vaccine Support Project under the Asia-Pacific Vaccine Access Facility.

(ii) Immediate steps were also taken in Georgia to mobilize the additional funding for COVID-19 response. Universal health coverage program spending increased by 20%. For citizens and residents of the country, all costs associated with testing, outpatient and inpatient treatment, and isolation ("COVID hotels") are covered by the state budget.

(iii) In Kazakhstan, in addition to reallocations made in the state budget, additional resources to cover the immediate spending actions were mobilized from the government reserve.

(iv) In Azerbaijan, necessary funding has been allocated to the State Agency for Compulsory Medical Insurance from the reserve fund of the President for the necessary medical equipment and other supplies to prevent the spread of COVID-19. The President created a special fund to support the fight against COVID-19 , with additional contributions from the public and private sectors.

(v) In Tajikistan, the government amended the 2020 state budget, substantially increased healthcare expenditure, and expanded social assistance transfers to the population (i.e., deferred tax payments, and postponed the administrative price increases, and provided liquidity support to firms and households).

Sources: ADB. CAREC National Assessment Report. Unpublished; ADB. 2018. *Investing in Regional Health Security for Sustainable Development in Asia and the Pacific.* Manila; ADB. 2021. *Report and Recommendation of the President to the Board of Directors: Proposed Loan Islamic Republic of Pakistan—COVID-19 Vaccine Support Project under the Asia Pacific Vaccine Access Facility.* Manila; KPMG. 2020. *Azerbaijan: Government and Institution Measures in Response to COVID-19.*

---

[25] With PIP PC support, the national epidemiological and laboratory surveillance systems, including clinical management system for SARS infection cases, data management, and risk assessment systems, were improved and maintained in the long term by each country. See World Health Organization. Pandemic Influenza Preparedness (PIP) Framework.

[26] ADB. 2018. *Investing in Regional Health Security for Sustainable Development in Asia and the Pacific.* Manila.

[27] R. Horton. 2020. COVID-19: What Have We Learned So Far? *The Lancet.* 396 (1789); The Lancet. 2020. CAMS Health Conference, *Conference Brief Introduction.* The Lancet-CAMS Health Conference (sciconf.cn).

20. **Human resource capacity.** CAREC countries face different challenges in human resources for health, such as an aging workforce; inappropriate staff mix and recruitment policies; urban–rural maldistribution and retention issues; substandard quality of education; weak enforcement of standards and accreditation; poor absorption capacity; poor career structure, especially for women; and substandard working environment (footnote 2). Capacity to plan and manage the health workforce at the national, institutional, and operational levels, especially during case surges, needs to be strengthened. This has been particularly true during the current pandemic, where human resources for health have been in short supply in all CAREC countries, considering significantly increased need for health personnel to manage the dramatic surge of COVID-19 cases. The shortage has been more pronounced for doctors—particularly intensive care unit doctors, infectious disease specialists, and primary care doctors—as compared with nurses (except for a few countries experiencing a severe shortage of nurses prior to the pandemic). This is often combined with low salaries paid to medical workers, weak management practices, high rates of staff turnover, and lack of adequate mental healthcare support for health personnel.[28]

21. **Surveillance and laboratory capacity.** Efforts are being made in CAREC countries to develop national and regional capacity to analyze and link data through the national surveillance systems, as well as to ensure intersectoral collaboration among human, animal, and plant health sectors. Capability to rapidly collect and analyze information from these sectors is challenging due to different information systems often used in these areas. The laboratory capacities and systems for laboratory quality assurance and standardization within and among countries are very mixed. For instance, some countries have high-quality standard reference laboratories that meet international requirements (like Georgia and its Lugar Center), while other countries in the CAREC region have far less stringent systems in place. Despite the progress achieved in the region, quality control and laboratory capacity to handle COVID-19 testing and analysis in a number of CAREC countries are still suboptimal, mainly constrained by poor infrastructure (footnote 2).

22. **Accessible supplies for capacity surges.** The quality, availability, and affordability of medicines are a major concern in the region, particularly the trade in substandard and fake medicines, and related over-the-counter sale and incorrect use, which contribute to the emergence of drug resistance. Insufficient pharmacovigilance systems add to the burden— regulatory work often takes place in isolation, without considering that a similar product or manufacturing site has been or is being assessed by several other countries. Limited competition in the markets has resulted in limited availability and higher prices (footnote 2). The noted weaknesses are largely due to significant volume of regulatory and administrative work being performed by authorities with weak institutional and human capacity, limited resources, and, at times, inadequate skills.

23. During the COVID-19 pandemic, many CAREC countries experienced significant delays in getting PPE, diagnostics, and vaccines due to a global gap in supplies and available stockpiles for urgently needed items. Many countries in the region, therefore, have limited preventive and curative surge capacity for emergencies.[29] This underlines the need and the potential for regional cooperation in terms of pooling resources for collaborative procurement, as well as for longer-term strategic partnership for building manufacturing capacity in the CAREC region. The Access to COVID-19 Tools Accelerator and

---

[28] ADB. CAREC National Assessment Report. Unpublished.

[29] V.S. Balakrishnan. 2020. COVID-19 Response in Central Asia. *The Lancet Microbe.* 1 (7). p. e281; E.M. Abrams and S.J. Szefler. 2020. COVID-19 and the Impact of Social Determinants of Health. *Lancet Respir Med.* 8 (7). pp. 659–661; A. Lal et al. 2021. Fragmented Health Systems in COVID-19: Rectifying the Misalignment between Global Health Security and Universal Health Coverage. *The Lancet.* 397 (10268). pp. 61–67.

COVID-19 Vaccines Global Access (COVAX), which are a global collaboration, have been launched to accelerate the development and manufacture of COVID-19 therapeutics, diagnostics, and vaccines and to guarantee fair and equitable access for every country in the world, including CAREC countries.[30]

24. **Health financing and social (financial) protection.** Communicable diseases can be expensive for patients who require financial protection that can be guaranteed through universal health coverage (UHC). Health emergencies, such as the outbreak of COVID-19, put significant pressure on the supply side as health systems come under stress. Access to quality and affordable health services is a significant pillar of social protection. According to the UHC index, nine of the 11 CAREC countries are scoring satisfactorily.[31] However, out-of-pocket payments remain relatively high in the CAREC region and restrict access to care, especially for vulnerable population groups.[32] Many migrants lack health insurance coverage.

25. Financial shortages are putting pressure on the healthcare systems.[33] Government health expenditure as a share of GDP has fallen tremendously in almost all CAREC countries due to market economy declines (footnote 33). While healthcare provision was free at the point of delivery and quite extensive prior to independence in Central Asian and Caucasus countries, as well as in Mongolia, decreased government spending increased the burden on the household. The financial burden on patients and health systems is increasing even more with the growing burden of noncommunicable diseases (NCDs).

26. During the COVID-19 pandemic, countries with policies that are closely aligned with UHC frameworks and global health security have generally fared better and might be better equipped to recover after COVID-19, compared with countries with health systems that are not aligned to such frameworks.[34] Limited benefit packages of health insurance schemes in most CAREC countries and high out-of-pocket payments for many necessary services have posed a serious threat, especially to the most vulnerable population groups, during the pandemic (footnote 15).

27. **Service delivery and quality of care.** A key challenge in health service delivery is overburdened hospital services during outbreaks. Primary care remains too weak to handle even mild cases during disease outbreaks such as COVID-19, even though investments in producing family medicine and primary health care (PHC) doctors and nurses have been made over the past years (footnote 2). This is aggravated by the inability to scale up laboratory capacity on a timely basis to meet outbreak needs. The quality of care, especially in rural areas, remains substandard and affects overall health systems performance due to several issues. These issues include poor national alignment of protocols and practices with international evidence-based medicine, poor training of healthcare workers or absence of special education programs and modules, a lack of quality management, and insufficient investments in and maintenance of facilities (footnote 2). Especially during outbreaks such as COVID-19, adequate clinical governance is needed to deliver standardized and quality clinical services for patients. To control the spread of infections in facilities and protect healthcare workers, WHO strongly recommends implementation of relevant IPC measures, including at the primary care level, such as evidence-based, facility-adapted IPC guidelines and standard operating procedures (SOPs), ensuring proper practice of hand hygiene, decontamination of medical devices and patient

---

[30] World Health Organization. 2021. *Working for Global Equitable Access to COVID-19 Vaccines.* COVAX.

[31] World Health Organization. 2021. *Global Health Observatory.*

[32] K. Xu et al. 2003. Household Catastrophic Health Expenditure: A Multicountry Analysis. *The Lancet.* 362 (9378).

[33] B. Rechel et al. 2012. Lessons from Two Decades of Health Reform in Central Asia. *Health Policy and Planning.* 27. pp. 281–287.

[34] A. Lal et al. 2021. Fragmented Health Systems in COVID-19: Rectifying the Misalignment between Global Health Security and Universal Health Coverage. *The Lancet.* 397 (10268). pp. 61–67.

care equipment, environmental cleaning, healthcare waste management, and injection safety. Many of these are not adhered to or implemented adequately in the region, including in border areas.[35]

28. **Supportive digital health.** Digital health is critical to addressing public health threats. It can, for instance, support surveillance and laboratory information systems for detection, help manage human resources and logistics of supplies during case surges, or support telemedicine services for improving care or providing essential services during outbreaks. Digital health and information systems have moved higher in the agenda of most CAREC countries. However, challenges still exist, such as fragmentation of information systems, a lack of national digital health strategies, and insufficient use of data for decision making. National health information systems in the CAREC region are typically fragmented due to parallel disease surveillance systems; lack of integration of the private sector; and fragmentation between facilities at the national, provincial, and local levels (footnote 2).

29. **Driving innovation.** Driving innovation, even during times of crisis, is critical in supporting response, and requires a facilitative innovation ecosystem in place. The current COVID-19 pandemic has highlighted how innovative solutions can contribute to solving a health crisis. Since early 2020, numerous governments, organizations, companies, and academic institutions have rapidly developed innovative solutions to manage the COVID-19 crisis.[36] Global solutions have included initiatives on prevention (e.g., surveillance, tracking

and tracing, research collaborations), on managing services (e.g., new management guidelines), or on improving physical infrastructure (e.g., inexpensive ventilators, color-coded hospital treatment areas to identify COVID-19 and non-COVID-19 zones). Numerous innovation trackers and repositories have appeared, which provide overviews of specific fields of innovation.

30. Many innovative solutions have been implemented in CAREC countries in response to COVID-19, albeit so far mainly at national level, a selection of which is provided in Box 2.[37]

31. Besides health systems capacity, other factors such as urbanization, environment, and climate change, as well as migration and increased connectivity, are key drivers of regional health security threats.

32. **Urbanization, environment, and climate.** Urbanization, environmental factors, and climate change also play an important role as drivers of infectious diseases.[38] Climate change is having a widespread knock-on effect on vital sectors of economy and sustainable development of CAREC countries, including human health and environment (e.g., growing antimicrobial resistance, frequent disasters triggered by natural hazard), which poses a threat to regional health security.[39] While in countries like the PRC, Kazakhstan, or Uzbekistan, nearly 100% of the population can access safe drinking water, the percentage in Afghanistan is as low as 67%. The lack of access to sanitation also poses a serious health threat to some CAREC countries by increasing nosocomial

---

[35] World Health Organization. 2019. *Minimum Requirements for Infection Prevention and Control Programmes.* Geneva; ADB. 2021. *COVID-19 Vaccine Support Project under the Asia Pacific Vaccine Access Facility: Report and Recommendation of the President — Due Diligence on Hazardous Healthcare Waste Management.* Manila; O. Khan. 2010. Injection Safety in Central Asia. Thesis. Atlanta: Georgia State University.

[36] M. Merten. 2020. Public Health Innovations for COVID-19: Finding, Trusting and Scaling Innovation. *ADB Sustainable Development Working Paper Series.* No. 70. Manila: ADB.

[37] All innovations in CAREC countries are included in the ADB compilation of innovative responses to COVID-19.

[38] UNDP. 2020. *Addressing Climate Change and Health in the Europe and Central Asia Region: A Joint Value Proposition and Service Offering.* New York.

[39] CAREC Institute. 2020. *Policy Brief. Regional Climate Cooperation.* Urumqi; ADB. 2018. *Investing in Regional Health Security for Sustainable Development in Asia and the Pacific.* Manila.

Box 2: Innovative Solutions in the Fight Against COVID-19 in the CAREC Region

(i) The Ministry of Transport, Communication and High Technologies of the Republic of Azerbaijan, together with the United Nations Development Programme (UNDP) and SUP VC, an accelerator program, initiated the "Hack COVID-19: Global Virtual Hackathon" to crowdsource tech solutions to help people cope with the coronavirus crisis.

(ii) The People's Republic of China has been particularly active in coming up with innovative solutions around COVID-19, such as isolation and quarantine, by using drones for medical and biological materials and using telemedicine in rural areas to increase access to healthcare.

(iii) The Astana Civil Service Hub, a virtual alliance of practitioners for the exchange of experience in the context of COVID-19, helped apply innovations and best-fitting solutions to respond to the pandemic. The proposal for establishing the Regional Hub of Civil Service as a multilateral platform to reform civil services has been inspired by the Agency of Civil Service Affairs of the Republic of Kazakhstan jointly with UNDP in Kazakhstan.

(iv) The State Agency on Information and Communication Technology and the High Technology Park of the Kyrgyz Republic and UNDP established the "Inno4Kg-Innovation for Kyrgyz Republic" contest, which was expected to generate speedy, diverse, and effective solutions designed to tackle the cascading effects of COVID-19 and address the acute needs of vulnerable populations. The challenge was part of the joint humanitarian response under the Disaster Response Coordination Unit, established upon the request of the Government of the Kyrgyz Republic, to assist COVID-19 emergency preparedness and response and set the stage for early recovery.

(v) The Government of Mongolia developed a web portal through its Communication, Information, and Technology Agency to provide around 180 types of social services to Mongolians. Among others, the platform offers test results for COVID-19 and provides COVID-19 vaccine certificates.

(vi) Pakistan's Aga Khan University, Faculty of Health Sciences developed a repository of research projects related to COVID-19. In addition, the Sindh provincial government in Pakistan used an innovative tool that provided decision makers access to need-based, real-time, and high-resolution analytics and visualizations. The Sindh provincial government integrated 12 data sources into a virtual control room to improve situational awareness and enable a rapid, data-driven, and effective response to the outbreak. Decision makers used the virtual control room to make informed decisions about where to send patients in need of critical care; optimize the allocation of lifesaving resources, such as personal protective equipment and ventilators; and implement targeted lockdowns to control the spread of the virus. The platform is now being used to strengthen the delivery of routine immunization across Sindh.

(vii) The UN Special Programme for the Economies of Central Asia (SPECA), in the form of its Working Group on Innovation and Technology for Sustainable Development, has launched a project on strengthening innovation policies for SPECA countries in support of the 2030 Agenda for Sustainable Development. A first step of this new approach was an assessment of SPECA countries on gaps in innovations.

Sources: EU 4 Digital. 2020. *HACK COVID-19*; Astana Civil Service Hub. 2021. *Virtual Alliance of Practitioners for Exchange of Experience in the Context of the COVID-19*; UNDP. 2020. *UNDP Calls on Kyrgyz Innovators to Crack COVID-19 with Novel Solutions and Technology*; E-Mongolia Communication and Information Technology Department. 2021. *E-Mongolia*.

infections (and, with it, increasing antimicrobial resistance).[40] In Afghanistan and Pakistan, there is room for improvement (footnote 2). Considering that livestock production is an important contributor to local economies and an important part of cross-border trade, this region is particularly vulnerable to zoonotic diseases outbreaks that may continue to occur in the future (footnote 2).

33. **Migration and increasing connectivity.** Increased connectivity along cross-border economic corridors, such as the Almaty–Bishkek Economic Corridor (ABEC) and urbanizing economic clusters, requires sufficient infrastructure and access to health services for migrant and mobile populations, sound capacity for detection of infectious disease outbreaks, IPC in facilities, and quarantine facilities. Labor migration constitutes a major health determinant because increased mobility increases the risk for infectious diseases crossing borders. In 2019, around 10.3 million migrants from CAREC countries worked outside their home countries (footnote 39). Social protection for labor migrants

is mostly missing, and either facilities in border areas are scarce or access to healthcare for labor migrants does not exist at all. Thus, labor migrants are especially prone to health hazards. The incidence of TB and MDR-TB is 2.5 times higher among labor migrants than among the general population.[41] The number of documented migrants is presented in Table 2.

34. Female migrant workers in the CAREC region and from the region working elsewhere represent a particularly vulnerable group, often exposed to a multitude of risks. Their needs are poorly reflected by national health statistics since these women often fall outside the available services and therefore do not appear visibly in the statistics. Since a significant proportion of female population in all CAREC countries work abroad as migrant workers, the ambition to meet their health needs warrants attention. Design and launch of supportive initiatives to meet the health needs of female migrant workers need investigations to define their actual needs. So far, this has only been highlighted in a very limited range of published studies.

Table 2: International Migrant Stock in CAREC Countries, 2019

Indicators	AFG	AZE	PRC	GEO	KAZ	KGZ	MON	PAK	TAJ	TKM	UZB
Number of migrants[a] ('000)	150	254	1,031	79	3,706	200	21	3,258	274	195	1,168
Migrants as % of national population	0.4	3	0.1	2	20	3	0.7	2	3	3	4
Female migrants as % of all migrants	50	52	39	56	50	60	33	47	57	53	53
Type of data[b]	B	B, R	C	B	B	B	C	B, R	B	B	B

AFG = Afghanistan, AZE = Azerbaijan, CAREC = Central Asia Regional Economic Cooperation, GEO = Georgia, KAZ = Kazakhstan, KGZ = Kyrgyz Republic, MON = Mongolia, PAK = Pakistan, PRC = People's Republic of China, TAJ = Tajikistan, TKM = Turkmenistan, UZB = Uzbekistan.

[a] Totals are only an estimate as the number of informal migrants cannot be accurately counted.

[b] This row indicates the data used to produce the estimates: (B) foreign-born population, (C) foreign citizens, and (R) refugees.

Sources: United Nations Department of Economic and Social Affairs. International Migration (accessed 16 January 2020); ADB. 2021. *Toward CAREC 2030: Enhancing Regional Cooperation in the Health Sector—A Scoping Study.* Manila.

---

[40] Center for Strategic and International Studies (CSIS). 2021. *WASH as a Critical Component of Primary Health Care and Health Security.*

[41] B. Babamuradov et al. 2017. Reducing TB Among Central Asia Labor Migrants. *Health Aff (Millwood).* 36 (9). p. 1688.

35.   Three factors increasing the population's vulnerability to health security threats have been identified. These are gender inequities, social determinants of health, and the high burden of NCDs.

36.   **Gender inequities.** Several assessments conducted during the first months of the COVID-19 pandemic revealed that gender inequality has increased throughout the health crisis.[42] There has been an increase in domestic/gender-based violence.[43] Women could not access health services as frequently as prior to the crisis. Besides, decreased working hours of women resulted in decreased earnings and subsequent difficulties in affording basic expenses such as utilities and rent. In addition, a large proportion of health workers in the CAREC region are women, which makes women particularly vulnerable to infectious disease threats. Given the impact on women, gender-sensitive measures need to be in place to protect them.

37.   **Social determinants of health.**[44] The COVID-19 pandemic has demonstrated how poverty and social inequality can increase vulnerability to infectious disease outbreaks and spread, as follows: (i) social inequalities in health have impacted COVID-19 mortality and morbidity,[45] (ii) the disease has widened the gap between rich and poor, and (iii) households from lower income groups are at higher risk of viral transmission because of crowded living spaces and lesser access to health infrastructure.[46]

38.   CAREC countries have substantially reduced their poverty rates due to several factors, including relatively high economic growth and improvement of social services. However, the poverty rate remains high in Afghanistan, at 54.5%, and Tajikistan, at 26.3%.[47] CAREC countries vary significantly in terms of state fragility and social safety nets to protect their citizens. The 2018 UN Human Development Index of CAREC countries ranged from 0.496 for Afghanistan to 0.817 for Kazakhstan, while the inequality-adjusted Human Development Index ranged from 0.386 for Pakistan to 0.759 for Kazakhstan (data on Afghanistan is not available).[48] Given this situation, investing in social protection schemes and capacity is critical in protecting the population from adverse impacts of disease outbreaks.

39.   **Increased susceptibility to infectious diseases due to NCD burden.**[49] The COVID-19 pandemic has, furthermore, underlined that co-morbidity with NCDs can make populations more vulnerable to morbidity and mortality from

---

[42] UNDP. 2016. *Gender Assessments in Europe and Central Asia Reveal Pandemic's Devastating Impact on Women;* World Bank. 2014. *Why We Care about Closing Gender Wage Gaps in the South Caucasus;* UN Women. 2020. *UN Women Series: Women at the Forefront of COVID-19 Response in Europe and Central Asia: Voices of Gender Equality Mechanisms on COVID-19.*

[43] UN Women. *The Shadow Pandemic: Violence Against Women During COVID-19.*

[44] Social determinants of health are the nonmedical factors that influence health outcomes such as income, education, and housing. They are the conditions in which people are born, grow, work, live, and age, and the wider set of forces and systems shaping the conditions of daily life. See WHO. Social Determinants of Health.

[45] E.M. Abrams and S.J. Szefler. 2020. COVID-19 and the Impact of Social Determinants of Health. *Lancet Respir Med.* 8 (7). pp. 659–661.

[46] A. Lal et al. 2021. Fragmented Health Systems in COVID-19: Rectifying the Misalignment between Global Health Security and Universal Health Coverage. *The Lancet.* 397 (10268). pp. 61–67.

[47] World Bank. Poverty Headcount Ratio at National Poverty Lines—Afghanistan, Tajikistan (accessed 12 December 2020).

[48] UNDP. Human Development Reports. Global Human Development Indicators (accessed 12 December 2020).

[49] Vulnerability to development of severe illness and risk of mortality among those infected with COVID-19 are well documented to be associated with NCDs, obesity, diabetes, and hypertension. Those conditions also lead the statistics over premature mortality in Central Asia. See Institute for Health Metrics and Evaluation. 2018. *Global Burden of Disease Study Results, 2017.* Seattle, Washington. http://ghdx.healthdata.org/gbd-results-tool (accessed December 2019); CDC. 2021. Underlying Medical Conditions Associated with High Risk for Severe COVID-19: Information for Healthcare Providers.

infectious diseases. In the CAREC region, the burden of disease is dominated by NCDs even if CAREC countries are at various stages in their demographic and epidemiological transitions.[50] Some countries, like Afghanistan, Pakistan, and Tajikistan, are still facing a high share of the population dying from infectious diseases and a growing share of the population dying from NCDs (Figure 2).[51]

40. Cardiovascular diseases are among the most common NCDs in CAREC countries. Unmet needs to manage risks in case management of cardiovascular diseases are driving the stroke and cardiovascular prevalence and mortality rates

across CAREC.[52] The transition toward modern cardiovascular disease management—including the use of effective PHC, continuous follow-up, and active promotion of life-long compliance with daily treatment—is not well supported due to a strong tradition of hospital-centric care. While this strategy focuses on health security, investing in addressing NCDs will remain critical across the region.

41. **Summary.** Based on the above-described analysis, a problem tree analysis was conducted to analyze the causes and effects of the pandemic situation in CAREC countries (Figure 3).

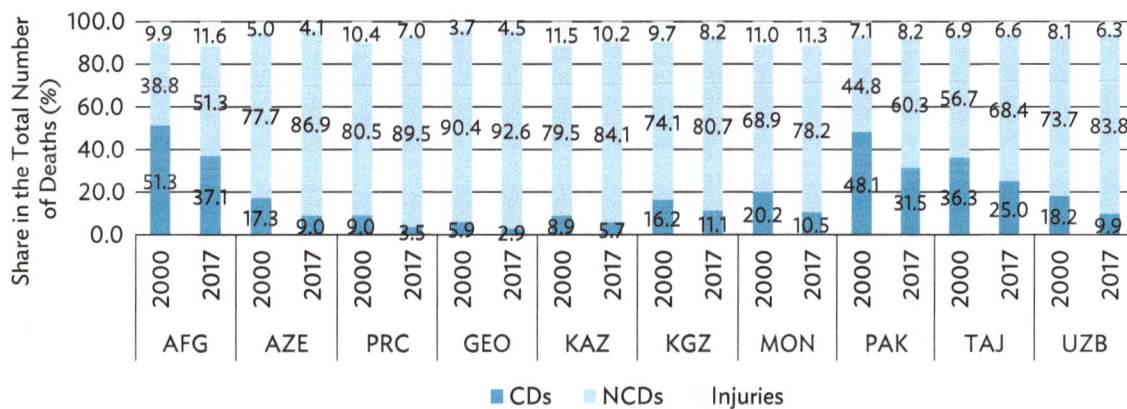

Figure 2: Burden of Disease in CAREC Countries

AFG = Afghanistan, AZE = Azerbaijan, CD = communicable disease, GEO = Georgia, KAZ = Kazakhstan, KGZ = Kyrgyz Republic, MON = Mongolia, NCD = noncommunicable disease, PAK = Pakistan, PRC = People's Republic of China, TAJ = Tajikistan, UZB = Uzbekistan.

Source: Institute for Health Metrics and Evaluation. 2018. Global Burden of Disease Study Results, 2017. Seattle, Washington. healthdata.org (accessed December 2019).

---

[50] Mortality and morbidity from infectious diseases is declining and mortality and morbidity from NCDs is increasing (footnote 2). In principle, this means that noncommunicable diseases, communicable diseases, reproductive health-related diseases, and injuries exist, though in varying degrees.

[51] World Bank Open Data Indicators. data.worldbank.org/indicator (accessed 10 August 2021).

[52] The key to reduce case fatality in stroke and cardiovascular disease (CVD) is through risk-factor-based UHC for cardiovascular disease management. This strategy has led to drastic reductions of CVD-associated stroke mortality and hypertension-associated CVD mortality during the past 20 years, in countries that have implemented a "Framingham-aligned" model of care.

Figure 3: Core Regional Health Problems for CAREC Countries

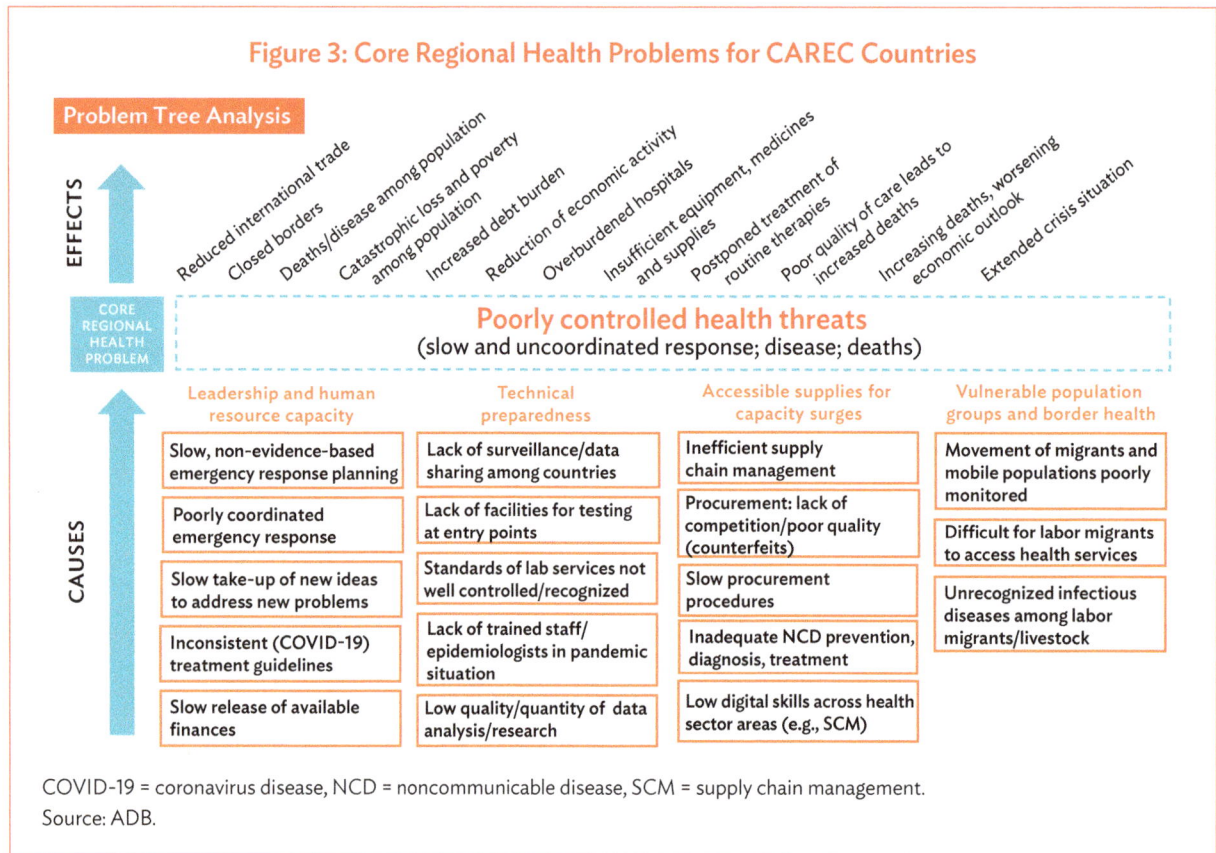

Problem Tree Analysis

EFFECTS

Reduced international trade · Closed borders · Deaths/disease among population · Catastrophic loss and poverty among population · Increased debt burden · Reduction of economic activity · Overburdened hospitals · Insufficient equipment, medicines and supplies · Postponed treatment of routine therapies · Poor quality of care leads to increased deaths · Increasing deaths, worsening economic outlook · Extended crisis situation

CORE REGIONAL HEALTH PROBLEM

Poorly controlled health threats
(slow and uncoordinated response; disease; deaths)

CAUSES

Leadership and human resource capacity	Technical preparedness	Accessible supplies for capacity surges	Vulnerable population groups and border health
Slow, non-evidence-based emergency response planning	Lack of surveillance/data sharing among countries	Inefficient supply chain management	Movement of migrants and mobile populations poorly monitored
Poorly coordinated emergency response	Lack of facilities for testing at entry points	Procurement: lack of competition/poor quality (counterfeits)	Difficult for labor migrants to access health services
Slow take-up of new ideas to address new problems	Standards of lab services not well controlled/recognized	Slow procurement procedures	Unrecognized infectious diseases among labor migrants/livestock
Inconsistent (COVID-19) treatment guidelines	Lack of trained staff/epidemiologists in pandemic situation	Inadequate NCD prevention, diagnosis, treatment	
Slow release of available finances	Low quality/quantity of data analysis/research	Low digital skills across health sector areas (e.g., SCM)	

COVID-19 = coronavirus disease, NCD = noncommunicable disease, SCM = supply chain management.
Source: ADB.

D. Opportunities for Regional Health Cooperation

42. Regional cooperation is essential in enhancing health security as a regional public good. Such cooperation can significantly facilitate implementation of IHR, as well as various regional frameworks to support countries in improving health security and addressing future public health threats (footnote 27). Some cooperation has already taken place among CAREC countries, for example through the RHC initiatives and projects that existed prior to the COVID-19 pandemic (Box 3).

43. CAREC countries are members of several regional groupings or bilateral agreements focusing on various health aspects (Box 4).

44. There are also several international initiatives in which some CAREC countries participate (Box 5).

45. The current pandemic has accelerated the initiation of new regional initiatives, for example, the UN Special Programme for the Economies of Central Asia (UN SPECA).[53] The regional platform is engaged in several sectors. In November 2020, countries came together to discuss and develop ideas for coordinated actions by governments, the UN system, and other relevant stakeholders to respond to the socioeconomic impacts of COVID-19. Afghanistan, Azerbaijan, Kazakhstan, the Kyrgyz Republic, Tajikistan, Turkmenistan, and Uzbekistan participated in the meeting. Another important platform for sharing experience and resources among CAREC countries are regional

---

[53] UNESCAP. 2020. *SPECA Economic Forum.*

hubs set up by WHO/Europe in Georgia and the Kyrgyz Republic, respectively.[54] The hubs' knowledge platforms ensure that WHO guidelines and tools are optimized according to each country's socioeconomic reality and needs. On-the-ground scientific assessments assist countries in developing their health systems and improving emergency preparedness, as well as in promoting intensive and fit-for-purpose activities in every aspect of public health.

46.   More research collaborations within CAREC are needed to create a stronger basis for outbreak response. The Eurasia Lab and Fellowship Programme, for instance, creates a major network of researchers, practitioners, and activists working on Eurasia.[55] Among others, the program organizes online workshops and public events to discuss the implication of the COVID-19 pandemic for researchers working on Eurasia. Azerbaijan, Georgia, Kazakhstan, the Kyrgyz Republic,

---

Box 3: Regional Health Cooperation Initiatives in CAREC Countries

(i)   Central Asia Regional Economic Cooperation (CAREC) sanitary and phytosanitary standards (SPS) modernization project—as part of the ongoing CAREC integrated trade facilitation and trade policy program to harmonize and upgrade SPS measures and facilitate trade in agriculture and food products within and beyond CAREC.

(ii)   Bilateral agreements for addressing TB/HIV epidemics in Kazakhstan, the Kyrgyz Republic, and Tajikistan, focusing on joint efforts in terms of design and implementation of the most effective TB and HIV prevention and care strategies in these neighboring countries.

(iii)   Improving hospital and laboratory infrastructure and capacity (e.g., strengthening laboratory capacity under the Almaty–Bishkek Economic Corridor, and construction of 50-bed hospital under the PRC–Pakistan Economic Corridor).

(iv)   Developing digital health solutions, such as e-learning and telemedicine projects at the Tajikistan, Pakistan, and the Kyrgyz Republic borders.

(v)   The Afghanistan and Pakistan partnership for the Polio Eradication Programme (public–private partnerships led by the governments) is spearheaded by partners such as the World Health Organization (WHO), the UN Children's Fund (UNICEF), the Bill & Melinda Gates Foundation, Rotary International, and the US Centers for Disease Control and Prevention.

Source: ADB. 2021. *Toward CAREC 2030: Enhancing Regional Cooperation in the Health Sector—A Scoping Study.* Manila.

Box 4: Regional Health Agreements and Groupings

(i)   The Regional Environmental Center for Central Asia

(ii)   Shanghai Cooperation Organization

(iii)   South Asia Association for Regional Cooperation

(iv)   Organization of the Black Sea Economic Cooperation

(v)   Commonwealth of Independent States

(vi)   Organization for Islamic Cooperation

Source: ADB. National Assessment Report. Unpublished.

---

[54]   World Health Organization, Europe. 2020. *WHO Hubs Pool Resources in the European Region to Boost COVID-19 Response.*

[55]   Institut für Europäische Politik. 2021. *Eurasia Lab and Fellowship Programme.* Berlin.

Box 5: International Initiatives

(i)   Select Central Asia Regional Economic Cooperation (CAREC) countries (Pakistan, Kazakhstan, Georgia, and Azerbaijan) have endorsed and implemented the One Health approach—an approach for collaboration of sectors for infectious diseases control that was introduced by the World Organization for Animal Health and WHO.[a] It is based on understanding risks for human and animal health (including both domestic animals and wildlife) and ecosystems.

(ii) Some CAREC countries (Afghanistan, Azerbaijan, PRC, Georgia, Kazakhstan, the Kyrgyz Republic, Mongolia, Pakistan, Tajikistan, and Uzbekistan) have implemented the Field Epidemiology Training Program (FETP), which is supported by the Training Programs in Epidemiology and Public Health Interventions Network (TEPHINET) amongst other.[b] FETP focuses on applied epidemiology, disease surveillance, outbreak response, and program evaluation with additional courses in study design and scientific writing. Some include a laboratory component. While enrolled, residents continue working in their respective countries' health systems and are well-positioned to serve as first responders to outbreaks and as leaders and mentors for future in-country specialists in field epidemiology.

(iii) The Coalition for Epidemic Preparedness Innovations (CEPI) has launched a new call to accelerate the development of a new vaccine. CEPI, a product development partnership, is an excellent example of the power of collaboration at the policy level and increased forces through joint efforts.

(iv) The global COVAX initiative has also been established to provide vaccines to developing countries.

[a] **World Health Organization.** One Health. One Health is defined as "an approach to designing and implementing programmes, policies, legislation and research in which multiple sectors communicate and work together to achieve better public health outcomes. The areas of work in which a One Health approach is particularly relevant include food safety, the control of zoonoses (diseases that can spread between animals and humans, such as flu, rabies, and Rift Valley Fever), and combatting antibiotic resistance (when bacteria change after being exposed to antibiotics and become more difficult to treat."

[b] **TEPHINET.** Central Asian Field Epidemiology Training Program. TEPHINET is a professional network of 73 field epidemiology training programs, including those with laboratory and veterinary components, working across more than 100 countries.

[c] **CEPI** is funded by Australia, Canada, Germany, Japan, Norway, the Bill & Melinda Gates Foundation, and the Wellcome Trust, among others. See Coalition for Epidemic Preparedness Innovations. CEPI.net (accessed July 2021).

Source: ADB. National Assessment Report. Unpublished.

Tajikistan, Turkmenistan, and Uzbekistan are members of the program. The program could serve as a role model for more joint approaches among CAREC countries.

47.   A review of national health policies (i.e., respective laws, regulations, plans, and strategies) in CAREC member countries clearly demonstrates national governments' support to health cooperation and global health partnerships (Appendix 3). This is, among others, evidenced by their commitments for international cooperation on the implementation of IHR and WHO Framework Convention of Tobacco Control (FCTC).

48.   As stated above, some subregional and cross-border initiatives exist, shown in several national strategies. The CAREC region does not have a common strategic approach for improving health security yet.[56] RHC is an opportunity for countries to jointly strengthen health security and achieve better outcomes. Focusing on key areas such as response to emergency public health threats; human resource capacity; procurement and supply management; digital health solutions; and coverage and quality of health services, including for women and vulnerable groups (e.g., the elderly, migrants, persons with disabilities, and people at excess risk due to preexisting comorbidities), are steps to achieving this goal.

---

[56] V.S. Balakrishnan. 2020. COVID-19 Response in Central Asia. *The Lancet Microbe.* 1 (7). p. e281; E.M. Abrams and S.J. Szefler. 2020. COVID-19 and the Impact of Social Determinants of Health. *Lancet Respir Med.* 8 (7). pp. 659–661; A. Lal et al. 2021. Fragmented Health Systems in COVID-19: Rectifying the Misalignment between Global Health Security and Universal Health Coverage. *The Lancet.* 397 (10268). pp. 61–67.

4

CAREC HEALTH STRATEGY 2030

A. Vision

49.   The proposed vision of the CAREC Health Strategy 2030 is "Public health threats in the CAREC region are addressed comprehensively, efficiently, and sustainably through adopting a regional approach while safeguarding the needs of the most vulnerable segments of the population."

B. Guiding Principles

50.   **Regional health cooperation.** This is key for building more resilient health systems and effective health security across the region, such as responding to outbreaks like the COVID-19 pandemic. Cooperation can maximize the impact of interventions in health systems through taking advantage of and building on existing efforts and initiatives. It can happen at subregional level, with countries cooperating bilaterally, or in clusters, where countries share borders and/or common interests, given that the CAREC region is large and diverse. Regional health cooperation does not substitute national strategies and policies but rather complements national efforts for strengthening health systems, as well as improving health security. Health innovations and the need for effective health security as a basis for safe cross-border trade in goods and services can be leveraged as a driver for cooperation. The following guiding principles will underpin the development of CAREC health cooperation initiatives and programs and the promotion of health cooperation in the region.

51.   **Fostering multisector coordination.** Multisector collaboration promotes policy and research across multiple sectors communicating and working together to achieve public health outcomes. The COVID-19 response demonstrated that several ministries and actors had to be involved in deciding on adequate response measures, and in many countries, interagency coordination platforms were set up. Multisector coordination also requires close coordination with various stakeholders, such as academia, civil society organizations, and the private sector.

52.   To effectively manage a One Health approach, multisector coordination is needed as part of a holistic viewpoint of health that covers factors related to the environment, sanitary and phytosanitary, and the risk for spillover of infectious diseases between humans and animals.[57]

53.   **A clear focus on benefiting the population,** especially migrants and others who are most vulnerable and may not be able to afford high healthcare costs, or find it difficult to access timely and quality health services for reasons such as geographical location, gender, age, income, or ethnicity, especially at the primary care level.[58] CAREC health initiatives will be constantly monitored for their impact, with appropriate adjustments made, if needed, to maximize benefits to the population, including the most vulnerable segments and special needs of women.

54.   **Ensuring feasibility and an evidence-based approach** promotes the high probability and value of successful implementation. Gap or needs assessments should guide the strategic direction of regional project design by ensuring that each step is based on evidence and the reality on the ground. Pilot testing of new approaches that have not yet been tested or proven globally or in the region will boost innovation and learning.

55.   **Safeguarding sustainability and ownership.** The CAREC Health Strategy 2030 seeks to support initiatives and cooperation that focus on the potential for long-term, cost-effective, and continual achievement of worthwhile results. It further aims for alignment with national priorities while supporting advancement of regional health cooperation in areas where it adds value and

---

[57]   The One Health approach is relevant in antimicrobial resistance, which requires close collaboration across sectors, stakeholders, and countries.

[58]   ADB. 2011. *Sectoral Perspectives on Gender and Social Inclusion.* Manila.

complements national strategies and programs. Sustainable development cooperation occurs when there is national (cooperative) ownership of the initiatives and is enhanced when existing initiatives are built on or leveraged. A phased approach or a gradual development of regional health cooperation in CAREC helps build understanding and ownership and allows lessons learned from one phase to translate into greater achievements in the next.

56. **Alignment with international policies and frameworks**, such as those established under WHO and other recognized global health organizations, will ensure that the CAREC Health Strategy synergizes and enhances global health initiatives. Such international policies include the IHR, WHO FCTC, and the NCDs Global Monitoring Framework.[59] It further includes the principles of the Helsinki declaration on the human rights of the patient, ethical rules in epidemiology, and the World Medical Association resolution on implementation of WHO FCTC on ethical considerations regarding health databases as complement to the Declaration of Helsinki.[60] The strategy also needs to align with UN development goals and commitments of UN High-Level Meetings, for instance, the 2030 Sustainable Development Goals (SDG) and UN High-Level Meeting of UHC.

C. Strategic Framework

57. The framework for the CAREC Health Strategy (Figure 4) is derived from the analysis of the core issues impeding regional health cooperation and security. The analysis is drawn from desk research, findings from the scoping

study, feedback received from member countries and development partners during the virtual regional consultation meetings, and preliminary results from the national assessments. Based on the ideas formulated by the CAREC WGH and the analysis of the core issues aggravating regional health security, a strategic framework for the CAREC Health Strategy 2030 was developed. To achieve the overall vision, the CAREC Health Strategy identifies four pillars, as follows::

(i)   leadership and human resource capacity,
(ii) technical preparedness,
(iii) access to supplies and surge capacity, and
(iv) vulnerable population groups and border health.

58. The implementation of these pillars can be supported when several enabling factors are in place and relevant aspects of WHO-defined health system building blocks are covered.[61] The enabling factors for implementation include: (i) the necessary institutional setup, (ii) partnerships, and (iii) capacity support (Figure 4). Three crosscutting issues are described as part of the framework:

(i)   Digital health is the development, use, and scale-up of digital health technologies and solutions to improve health outcomes. This includes the utilization of a wider range of smart and connected devices, digital technologies such as the Internet of Things, virtual care, remote monitoring, artificial intelligence, big data analytics, blockchain, smart wearables, platforms, tools enabling data exchange and storage, remote data capture, and the exchange of data and sharing. Digital health should be supported by

[59]   World Health Organization. 2014. *Noncommunicable Diseases Global Monitoring Framework: Indicator Definitions and Specifications.* Geneva.

[60]   World Bank. 2019. *Why We Care about Closing Gender Wage Gaps in the South Caucasus;* T. Khitarishvili. 2016. Gender Dimensions of Inequality in the Countries of Central Asia, South Caucasus, and Western CIS. *Working Paper Series.* No. 858. New York: Levy Economics Institute of Bard College; UNICEF. 2016. *Rapid Review on Inclusion and Gender Equality in Central and Eastern Europe, the Caucasus and Central Asia.* Geneva; OECD. 2019. *Draft Background Note Promoting Gender Equality in Eurasia: Better Policies for Women's Economic Empowerment.* Paris.

[61]   World Health Organization. 2007. *Everybody's Business: Strengthening Health Systems to Improve Health Outcomes: WHO's Framework for Action.* Geneva.

Figure 4: CAREC Health Strategy Framework

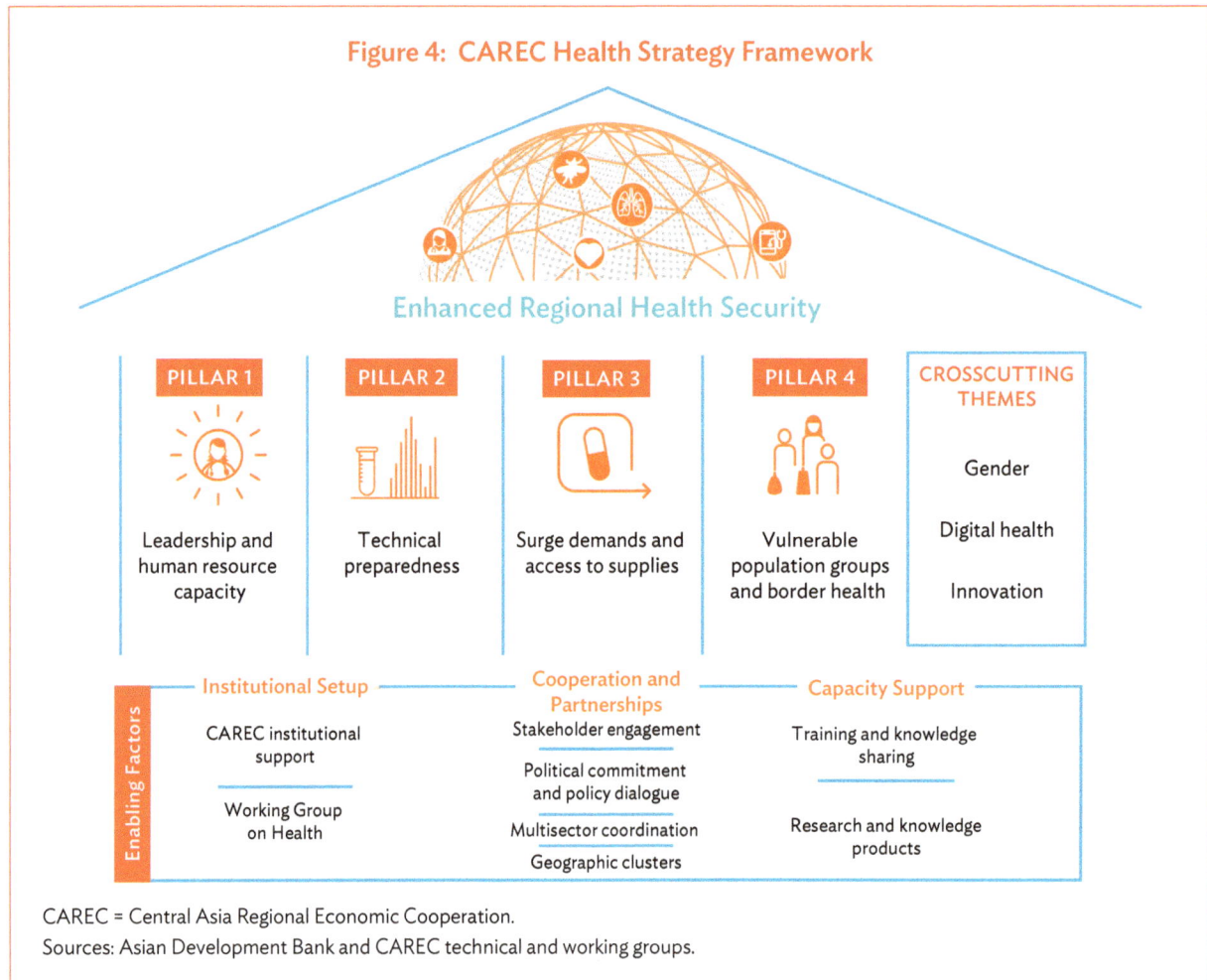

Enhanced Regional Health Security

PILLAR 1	PILLAR 2	PILLAR 3	PILLAR 4	CROSSCUTTING THEMES
Leadership and human resource capacity	Technical preparedness	Surge demands and access to supplies	Vulnerable population groups and border health	Gender / Digital health / Innovation

Enabling Factors

Institutional Setup
- CAREC institutional support
- Working Group on Health

Cooperation and Partnerships
- Stakeholder engagement
- Political commitment and policy dialogue
- Multisector coordination
- Geographic clusters

Capacity Support
- Training and knowledge sharing
- Research and knowledge products

CAREC = Central Asia Regional Economic Cooperation.
Sources: Asian Development Bank and CAREC technical and working groups.

sufficient investment in governance, including e-health strategies and institutional and workforce capacity.[62]

(ii) Innovation, which can serve as key for prevention, physical infrastructure, health service provision, and policy. Sufficient technical capacity and know-how for adopting, implementing, and scaling up innovative models and solutions for supporting health systems across the CAREC region are needed for improving health security.

(iii) Gender equity, which ensures that women are treated and evaluated in an equitable way vis-a-vis men and ensures that their specific needs are accounted for. Gender-related challenges that hinder women's and girls' access to health services need to be assessed and addressed. Access to health services, especially to quality health services on secondary- and tertiary-level and specialty treatment facilities, is needed to empower women (footnote 4).

D. Strategic Pillars

59. Table 3 outlines the four pillars and provides strategic objectives for each, including the crosscutting issues. A full list of possible actions can be found in Appendix 1.

---

[62] World Health Organization. 2020. *Global Strategy on Digital Health, 2020–2025.* Geneva.

Table 3: Strategic Pillars and Objectives

Goal: Enhance regional health security			
Pillars			Strategic Objectives
1	Leadership and human resource capacity	1.1	**Coordination and Governance.** Improved interministerial and multisector policy coordination, international support, and health system governance capacity in the CAREC region to respond to epidemic and pandemic health threats.
		1.2	**Workforce Skills and Capacity.** Sufficient workforce skills and capacity, especially in public health emergency leadership, public health, epidemiology, and research, for planning and implementing effective measures and innovations in response to public health threats, including the current COVID-19 pandemic.
			Strategic Objectives
2	Technical preparedness	2.1	**Surveillance Response.** Effective surveillance response to public health threats, including the current COVID-19 pandemic (e.g., improve surveillance systems, explore regional dashboards with automated early warning system, and compile regionally aligned awareness-raising materials on communicable diseases).
		2.2	**Laboratory Infrastructure.** Sufficient laboratory infrastructure and management according to international quality and biosafety requirements.
			Strategic Objectives
3	Access to supplies and surge capacity	3.1	**Regulatory Mechanisms.** Effective regulatory mechanisms and standards for medications and supplies.
		3.2	**Procurement Mechanisms.** Efficient national and regional procurement mechanisms for medications and supplies.
		3.3	**Supply Chain Management.** Reliable supply chain management that assures sufficient supply/stocks for emergency situations.
			Strategic Objectives
4	Vulnerable population groups and border health	4.1	**Access.** Improved access to health services (including COVID-19 vaccination) and cross-border referrals.
		4.2	**Burden of Disease.** Decreased burden of communicable diseases among migrants, border communities, and vulnerable population groups.
		4.3	**Infection prevention and control (IPC).** Effective IPC measures in border regions to protect travelers and the population including for COVID-19 cases.
Crosscutting issues			Digital Health/Innovations
			Digital Health/Innovation. Sufficient health information systems; data management; regional knowledge sharing; and improved capacity to develop, implement, and utilize innovative digital technologies and solutions.
			Gender
			Gender. Disaggregation of data by gender; specific needs of women considered in planning and design of health services and infrastructure.

Source: ADB.

1. Pillar 1: Leadership and Human Resource Capacity

60. **Key challenges.** The current pandemic revealed critical gaps and challenges in many CAREC countries where there has been an uncoordinated response. Countries lacked a permanent rapid response team structure, had weak and poorly integrated systems for cross-sector information exchange, lacked strategic emergency risk assessment, and had insufficient emergency preparedness capacity at public health centers and at the hospital level (footnote 28). Coordination of regional health threats is thus key to reducing the impact of epidemiological crises since viruses do not halt at national borders. Reducing the speed of the rate of epidemic or pandemic propagation buys time for health systems to prepare; avoids unmanageable surges of patients; and allows available resources, such as in intensive care, to operate at efficient occupancy rates—thus saving lives.

61. Coordination leading to cooperation among CAREC countries has already happened sporadically during the COVID-19 crisis. The PRC, for example, supported many other CAREC countries with knowledge transfer and technology.[63] Kazakhstan helped Tajikistan facilitate the transport of goods and assisted Tajik citizens travel back to their home country. Uzbekistan supported Tajikistan and the Kyrgyz Republic in the delivery of PPEs (footnote 63). While communication approaches focused mainly on broadcast and media, risk communication and community engagement (RCCE) were not rapidly applied in most CAREC countries. Mongolia and the PRC placed a clear focus on keeping the public informed through daily updates to the nation and via text messages.[64] However, comprehensive risk communication was not yet in place.

62. Investments in human resource development are required to better meet the needs of CAREC countries in the health sector in terms of numbers of medical personnel, their knowledge, and their skills mix. To address human resource capacity gaps, efforts have been made by development partners in the region such as WHO and UN agencies, the World Bank, and the European Union (EU), which can be used as a foundation for further work. This will require the cooperation of development partners on shared priorities to build the capacity of the public health workforce. This includes a needs assessment about workforce gaps and training priorities to help inform decisions for workforce development, as well as promoting essential crosscutting skills to complement public health workers' discipline-specific skills.[65]

63. Training of other clinical personnel is also needed. This may include doctors, nurses, and relevant ancillary staff. Topics may focus on health security measures and up-to-date methods for the prevention of spread and management of cases. Special attention needs to be paid to female health workers, who often predominate lower ranks of the health workforce and thus are more prone to risks such as infection. Regional cooperation could be useful in sharing best practices in terms of training modules at the undergraduate or postgraduate level, including continuous professional development, and in developing regional e-learning courses on specific skills needed in the region. While planning and implementing the respective training programs in CAREC countries, careful consideration should be given to the regional context and dynamics, such as doctors' and patients' mobility across borders to access specialized medical services in neighboring countries, as well as availability of relevant institutions with advanced-level expertise that can serve as regional hubs for training of clinical personnel and public health professionals.

---

[63] Caspian Policy Center. 2020. *The Caspian Region and the U.S. Engagement During and After the COVID-19 Crisis.* Washington, DC.

[64] Prevent Pandemics. 2020. *COVID-19 in Mongolia;* R. Horton. 2020. COVID-19: What Have We Learned So Far? *The Lancet.* 396 (10265). p. 1789.

[65] Centers for Disease Control and Prevention (CDC). 2021. *Action Plan Public Health Workforce Development.*

64. Of particular importance to improving detection of infectious diseases are effective laboratory practices that produce accurate results. This depends on continuous supervision and medical education for mid-level health personnel, as well as for doctors, and updating and upgrading skills and procedural competencies in a coordinated way to ensure unified testing results. Existing regional initiatives (e.g., WHO/Europe PIP PC, and the Better Labs for Better Health initiative) and advanced-level laboratories (e.g., the Richard G. Lugar Center for Public Health Research in Georgia and the Public Health Research Laboratory in Kazakhstan) can provide further leadership and guidance for improving the skills of the laboratory workforce in the region.[66]

65. **Proposed actions.** Pillar 1 will focus on strengthening leadership and human resource capacity through promotion of a more coordinated response to emergency public health threats and support of workforce skills. Main areas of intervention may include the following:

(i) Improving interministerial and intersectoral coordination and governance in the CAREC region, including regional dialogue mechanisms; mapping the status quo of IHR; and knowledge and experience sharing among countries in the CAREC region.

(ii) Strengthening the technical capacity of policymakers, public health managers, and planners, as well as epidemiologists and data scientists in health policy; planning, managing, and implementing effective and gender-sensitive measures to respond to public health threats and emergencies, including the COVID-19 pandemic; enhancing resilience and pandemic preparedness through regional capacity building and knowledge sharing opportunities and platforms; and improving the leadership and governance skills of health policymakers regarding health emergencies.

(iii) Establishing and strengthening emergency operations centers (EOCs) in close collaboration with IHR focal points in member countries, providing a central location from which to coordinate data collection and response to public health threats at the national level, and supporting exchange and networking among regional EOCs to strengthen the coordinated response.[67]

(iv) Strengthening joint outbreak response among CAREC countries; supporting them in carrying out health emergency drills and cooperation; and exploring cooperation with CAREC countries on core capacity building at points of entry under International Health Regulations (2005).

(v) Improving the distribution of the health workforce in CAREC countries (e.g., by preparing capacity development plans for rural areas).

(vi) Strengthening the knowledge and skills of the public health and epidemiological workforce (male and female), including mid-level health professionals (e.g., lab-technicians), through regional webinars; and recommending skills-focused, continuous medical training modules specifically targeting laboratory operations and methods, laboratory quality assurance and quality control, laboratory biosafety, and evidence base for epidemic countermeasures to control and contain key regional health threats.

(vii) Improving technical skills for early warning, alert, and response in emergencies; supporting CAREC member countries in the development of field-based tools (includes online, desktop, and mobile application that can be rapidly configured and deployed); and conducting training programs that include female participants.

(viii) Further exploring of options and possible piloting to implement pandemic risk financing.

---

[66] World Health Organization. 2018. *Better Labs for Better Health: Strengthening Laboratory Systems in WHO European Region.* Geneva; CDC. 2019. *Georgia: A Neutral Hub Brings Disease Detectives Together;* Global Biodefense. 2014. *BSL 3 Research Laboratory Opens in Kazakhstan.*

[67] Center for Strategic and International Studies. *Polio Emergency Operations Centers.* https://www.csis.org/features/polio-emergency-operations-centers (accessed July 2021).

(ix) Improving research and appropriate best practice results on communicable and noncommunicable diseases, especially from within the region, promoted through relevant regional research training opportunities, including study reports and webinars, provided by regional and international agencies.

2. Pillar 2: Technical Preparedness

66. **Key challenges.** There is a need to improve coordinated response through regional alignment in planning and implementing measures in response to public health threats, including the current COVID-19 pandemic. During emergencies, existing national public health surveillance systems may be underperforming, disrupted, or nonexistent, or they may become overwhelmed without an early warning system to detect and react rapidly to suspected disease outbreaks. Evidence from national data shows vast differences in how many tests are conducted per 100,000 people across CAREC member countries, as well as vast differences in national capacity for polymerase chain reaction (PCR) testing and ability to keep surveillance testing capacity in line with escalating pandemic developments. National results from PCR testing show how the daily rate of positive tests runs high, up to and above 20% to 30% in episodes during the past years in several CAREC countries.[68] Increase in the daily rate of positive tests shows that the reported number of confirmed cases only represents a minor proportion of the total number infected, and consequently, there is a need to expand testing. WHO recommends testing volumes to be expanded, so daily rates of positive tests will not exceed 5%.

67. Given the high rate of positive PCR tests, only a small portion of infected are caught by the surveillance sampling and testing. That leaves a huge proportion of the pandemic undetected. This makes calculations of needed healthcare resources from surveillance data impossible. Differences in proportion of infections detected and several other complications due to significant inter- and intra-country differences in surveillance sampling, principles for selection of cases to test, and choice of methods for analysis make comparisons of epidemiological statistics between CAREC countries difficult. Therefore, a data- and facts-driven coordinated action to control, mitigate, and contain the pandemic becomes very hard to formulate across CAREC countries.

68. A regionally synchronized planning and operation of surveillance, using the same methods for sampling and analysis, would thus be very helpful in enabling a regional "joint grip" on the extent of the COVID-19 challenge. Such a joint regional approach, with comparable data from countries, would help decision makers choose approaches to reduce risk from further spread of the disease. Cross-country access to and sharing of quality data is a critical prerequisite for guiding a coordinated response. This requires the development of proper data sharing platforms and data visualization tools, as well as supporting the respective capacity-building efforts.

69. Sufficient laboratory infrastructure is a critical element of enhanced surveillance and overall health systems capacity, particularly during pandemic threats. The COVID-19 pandemic revealed the need for a surge capacity plan by establishing decentralized testing capacity in subnational laboratories under the supervision of the national reference laboratory, if available.[69] This is illustrated by the WHO-recommended goal to stem epidemic spread by increasing the number of sampling and testing to keep the daily positive test rates below 2%. Using experience and statistical data from CAREC countries from the past year, planning for better surge capacity preparedness can be achieved.

---

[68] Our World in Data. ourworldindata.org (accessed 21 September 2021).

[69] World Health Organization. 2020. *Laboratory Testing Strategy Recommendations for COVID-19.*

70.   Results of the national assessments conducted in CAREC countries revealed critical gaps in different components of laboratory quality management systems (LQMS), such as quality control and assurance measures of national laboratory networks, insufficient specimen transport and referral, and lack of integration of and interoperability between the health and laboratory information systems, among others. All the components of the LQMS, including biosafety and biosecurity, equipment maintenance, quality control, quality assurance, external quality assurance, supply chain management with a specimen transport system, information management, personnel management, and professional development, must be functioning well to ensure that the country's laboratory system is capable in effectively responding to public health threats and emergencies. In addition, the pre-analytical part of laboratory testing, such as sample collection and the training of personnel involved in sample collection, even when not performed by the laboratory, needs to be considered.

71.   **Proposed actions.** Pillar 2 will focus on improving technical preparedness in the region. Areas of intervention may include the following:

(i)   Improving sharing of epidemic information according to IHR and in line with laws and regulations in respective CAREC member countries.

(ii)   Strengthening national and regional laboratory networks and laboratory systems for testing.[70] This includes improving the multifunctional equipment and methods for detecting potential pathogens; boosting PCR capacity and next-generation sequencing capacity; and establishing a Central Asian Regional Centre for Epidemiology, Virology and Bacteriology.[71]

(iii)   Exchanging strategies of sampling to enable cross-country comparisons, improve capacity for referral transport of specimens, and reduce turnaround time from sampling to result report, as well as capacity boosting for sensitivity and reliability through quality assurance and upgraded biosafety standards.

(iv)   Improving laboratory infrastructure and ensuring proper laboratory workflow and management according to international quality and biosafety requirements, including through existing regional initiatives and hubs.

(v)   Implementing support quality management systems (QMS) in laboratories through mentoring with trained national mentors.

3.   Pillar 3: Access to Supplies and Surge Capacity

72.   **Key challenges.** An efficient end-to-end supply chain is critical to delivering quality and affordable lifesaving medicines when and where they are needed. Supply chain management encompasses all activities required in acquiring and moving health products from manufacturer to user—from forecasting and procurement to storage and transport— considering the financial and information flows required to move the products through the supply chain. Reducing inefficiencies across the supply chain increases the quality and timing of service delivery while freeing up much-needed resources. In the CAREC region, such inefficiencies include limited competition in the market, leading to constrained supplies and higher prices. Many of these inefficiencies were amplified during the COVID-19 pandemic, bringing the long-standing vulnerability of medical supplies into sharp focus. Additionally, global shortages of medicines and supplies were experienced, and when they were available, the prices were very high and quality was not always assured.

73.   Inadequate regulatory mechanisms and enforcement result in delayed registration and importation of products while leaving the markets open to the entrance of poor-quality and falsified medicines. Poor data quality and lack of

---

[70]   A network is the physical number of laboratories and their served catchment areas, served facilities, or served populations. Laboratory systems include functionalities of reporting, quality assurance, and quality control mechanisms.

[71]   *Turkmenistan Golden Age News.* 2021. Central Asian Regional Center for Epidemiology, Virology and Bacteriology.

appropriate human resource capacity contribute to poor forecasting and supply-and-demand planning, resulting in imbalances in supply to meet the needs. Several gaps were revealed through the national assessments, including too centralized, very complex, and time-consuming procurement; limited supplier base; severe lack of medical oxygen at health facilities; insufficient electronic information systems to report stock-outs at health facilities in a timely manner; and lack of knowledge and capacity to respond to the pandemic in terms of prioritizing purchase of supplies and equipment.

74.   As COVID-19 spread across the globe, the demand outstripped medical supplies such as PPE, diagnostic tests, and ventilators. The supply became even more constrained with nationalist behaviors locking in manufacturing capacity and restricting the exportation of key raw materials.[72] Supply chains are failing at all levels. Centralized storage for emergency products is absent in the CAREC region, and many countries lack sufficient and appropriate cold chain equipment (ultra-cold chain freezers and temperature monitors) to store and transport temperature-sensitive vaccines. Coordination, best practice sharing, and research could be better adopted across the CAREC region, providing visibility across the end-to-end supply chain to enable more informed supply and demand planning, ensuring product availability when and where it is needed.

75.   **Proposed actions.** Pillar 3 will focus on enhancing access to supplies and increasing capacity to meet surge demands in the region.[73] Areas of intervention may include the following:

(i)   Improving regulatory mechanisms, standards, and procedures for medicines, laboratory equipment, and supplies (e.g., through harmonizing policies and regulations for authorization, registration, and importation of products; and investing in regional cooperation mechanisms to strengthen regulatory capacity).

(ii)   Improving procurement activities (e.g., procurement policies and procedures, standardization of supplier base, contracting, and supplier performance management).

(iii)   Creating more competitive and efficient market mechanisms to increase supply and reduce prices for medicines and supplies.

(iv)   Improving visibility and management of end-to-end procurement and supply chain from manufacturer through consumption (i.e., regional coordination of procurement and supply chain management activities, alignment and harmonization of data standards, and sharing of information and insights).

(v)   Streamlining movement of medical goods in the region, especially during emergencies, through further research on movement of goods; exploring harmonization of importation and exportation of medicines and supplies; and standardization and sharing of product master data, supply base, and contracting processes.

(vi)   Developing procurement and supply management capacity among health policymakers and personnel in the health sector and aligning approach, training, and tools across the region.

(vii)   Developing a supply chain risk management plan.

(viii)   Improving supply and stocks for emergency situations, including use of virtual control rooms (e.g., situation rooms) and joint opt-in procurement mechanisms.

(ix)   Further developing options for regional manufacturing and stockpiles.

---

[72]   F.A. Miller et al. 2021. Vulnerability of the Medical Product Supply Chain: The Wake-up Call of COVID-19. *BMJ Quality and Safety*. 30 (4). pp. 331–335.

[73]   While surge capacity may also refer to human resource needs and facility capacity, the pillar focuses on medicines, supplies, and equipment.

4. Pillar 4: Vulnerable Population Groups and Border Health

76. **Key challenges.** The current pandemic has uncovered existing challenges for vulnerable population groups, be they the poor, the elderly, women, or migrants. Millions of migrants from CAREC countries work outside their home countries, and effective measures are needed to control the spread of infectious diseases when they cross borders. In addition, social protection for labor migrants is not comprehensive, so access to health care can be difficult. The lack of health insurance coverage for this group and increased inequalities has burdened them even more. The lack of accessibility to health services in border areas has broadened gaps for migrants, mobile populations, and border communities—affecting their health status.

77. Other critical gaps with important implications for migrants and mobile populations in the region include hospital bed shortages (e.g., due to the surge of COVID-19 cases) and insufficient legal frameworks and oversight mechanisms for quality improvement of COVID-19 services. The overall burden of communicable diseases like HIV and TB among vulnerable population groups has been an ongoing threat, which has not been sufficiently addressed in the past and has been even more neglected due to the pandemic. Delivering sexual and reproductive health services to women, girls, and victims of gender-based violence during the crisis also has proven to be a challenge for many countries. IPC, which is critical in border areas, is generally substandard in terms of health facilities due to poor infrastructure, lack of equipment, and insufficient policies and regulations.[74]

78. **Proposed actions.** The CAREC Health Strategy 2030 will focus on enhancing health services for migrant, border, and vulnerable population groups through increased health and social protection mechanisms. The strategy will also improve database on this target group and their health needs, and strengthen referral system to ensure continuity of care for migrants and border-crossing communities with communicable diseases. Areas of intervention may include the following:

(i) Research on the health needs of CAREC cross-border communities and mobile populations, including women and other vulnerable groups.
(ii) Improving accessibility of health services while avoiding financial hardship and providing referral options to enhance continuity of care, especially with regard to PHC, for labor migrants and mobile populations crossing borders in high numbers, with special consideration for women's health needs.
(iii) Improving quality of treatment for migrants with TB and HIV (e.g., exploring to expand existing agreements on eligibility of migrants for HIV and TB diagnosis) as well as providing care and treatment to willing CAREC countries.
(iv) Strengthening or expanding agreements that target portability of benefits for migrants.
(v) Improving IPC measures, including in hospitals and primary care facilities in border areas, such as evidence-based, facility-adapted IPC guidelines and SOPs.
(vi) Improving the infrastructure and technical capacity of testing and quarantine facilities in border areas and points of entry, including for COVID-19 patients, to protect travelers and the population.
(vii) Supporting the upgrading of health facility infrastructure in border areas and cross-border economic corridors.
(viii) Defining minimum package of actions in response to public health threats in border

---

[74] ADB. 2021. *Toward CAREC 2030: Enhancing Regional Cooperation in the Health Sector—A Scoping Study.* Manila; ADB. 2021. *COVID-19 Vaccine Support Project under the Asia Pacific Vaccine Access Facility: Report and Recommendation of the President—Due Diligence on Hazardous Healthcare Waste Management.* Manila; O. Khan. 2014. *Injection Safety in Central Asia.* Thesis. Atlanta: Georgia State University.

areas and points of entry, including (a) access to medical services, like diagnostic services; (b) access to equipment and personnel for transporting infected travelers to the appropriate medical facility; (c) surveillance activities; (d) risk communication and social mobilization; (e) environmental health (i.e., vector control, solid and liquid waste management, potable water, and general sanitation); and (f) data management and information exchange in close collaboration with WHO.

5. Crosscutting Issues: Gender, Digital Health, and Innovations

79. **Key challenges to gender.** Gender equality in the health sector requires much work in CAREC countries. Awareness of gender issues is rare (footnote 42). The pandemic has even deepened the challenges that had existed prior to the outbreak, such as accessing health services, unequal earnings and job opportunities, mental health issues, and domestic violence.

80. **Proposed actions.** The CAREC Health Strategy 2030 will focus on achieving greater attention to the health needs of women and considering women in designing services and analyzing data (footnote 4). Areas of intervention may include the following:

(i) Improving sex disaggregation of data in the health sector of the CAREC region through the application of the CAREC WGH program.
(ii) Informing about gender concepts, meanings, gaps, and implementation options in health projects.
(iii) Including specific needs of women in health planning and designing of services.

81. **Key challenges for digital health.** Digital health is a key innovation and has the capacity to revamp healthcare systems across the region,

including in public health, health security, and clinical services efficiency. Key challenges in this domain with respect to CAREC countries include the ethical aspects of medical data management to meet international conventions on patients' human rights, as well as challenges in terms of needed infrastructure, interoperability, governance, and leadership. CAREC countries are at differing stages of digital readiness and maturity. The pandemic has significantly stressed existing information and communication technology (ICT) resources in these countries and has shown the importance of creating a robust health information technology (IT) infrastructure to enable maximum connectivity in these countries.

82. The ability to keep tabs on hospital occupation, average bed days, and intensive care unit occupation helps managers plan where and how to boost capacity to meet a surge in demand, such as during a pandemic. Analyzing such electronic information in terms of how interventions and mitigation efforts result or fail in "flattening the curve" is vital for health security and pandemic management. At the same time, personal rights to confidentiality and patient human rights need to be protected in how these electronic information systems are constructed and used.[75] Limited ICT network and interoperability and the need for strong commitment to the development of digital health human resource capacity, policies, and other ICT infrastructure to implement digital technologies, however, remain a very real challenge.

83. To benefit from a wide variety of digital health tools and services, governments must decide on the sequencing of digital health development and implementation according to the needs of the country and/or region. With limited resources, the implementation of large-scale digital health projects that attempt to solve different medical, public health, health care financing, and social care issues is not feasible. As a joint effort to

---

[75] World Health Organization. 2012. *Legal Frameworks for e-Health: Global Observatory for e-Health Series.* Volume 5. Geneva; WHO. 2017. *WHO Guidelines on Ethical Issues in Public Health Surveillance.* Geneva; B. Riso et al. 2017. Ethical Sharing of Health Data in Online Platforms: Which Values Should Be Considered? *Life Sci Soc Policy.* 13 (1). p. 12.

improve structural instruments for digitalization, CAREC countries should seek opportunities to build shareable resources for digital health. Those resources could include data security and privacy guidelines, policy for the digital identity of residents (including migrants), and taxonomies and vocabularies for health data and data exchange. A shared network of digital health training and education institutions would also help in the capacity building of the CAREC region.

84. **Proposed actions.** The CAREC Health Strategy 2030 will focus on strengthening health information systems in the CAREC region and managing data jointly and more efficiently.[76] Areas of intervention may include the following:

(i) Identifying willing CAREC member countries' digital health priorities and assessing their digital health landscapes, as appropriate, to suggest and support implementation of suitable digital health solutions.

(ii) In partnership with willing CAREC member countries, conducting gaps assessment for achieving graded stepwise health system data interoperability. An example is identifying gaps currently hampering the ability of different health sector IT systems to "speak to each other," including between laboratory devices and applications (systems such as patient records and encounter registers), so that data can be accessed, exchanged, integrated, and cooperatively used in a coordinated manner within and across organizational, regional, and national boundaries to provide timely and seamless portability of information to optimize health security.

(iii) Based on the gap analysis, proposing health data exchange architectures, application interfaces, and standards that enable data to be accessed and shared appropriately and securely across the complete spectrum of care in willing CAREC member countries; and providing the necessary training when such

sharing is to take place within all applicable settings and with relevant stakeholders.

(iv) Launching practical experimental initiatives for regionally unified coding of health data for willing CAREC countries through CAREC-wide promotion of WHO-recommended International Classification of Disease ICD-10 (and upcoming ICD-11) and International Classification of Primary Care to help ensure cross-country compatible and comparable data in national health IT systems and databases.

(v) Engaging in regional policy dialogues and knowledge exchange where information on successful digital approaches and policies to address challenges can be exchanged and fostered between countries.

(vi) Promoting and strengthening capacity on standardized and interoperable health information systems to overcome separate vertical systems and overlapping sources of data.

(vii) Improving data management and data capture mechanisms, including quality of captured data capacity, analytical capacity, and presentation skills, in willing CAREC member countries.

(viii) Adopting methods to enable cross-border data sharing and use in willing CAREC member countries.

(ix) Strengthening digital leadership and digital skills among the top-level decision makers.

(x) Developing a sustainable and realistic regional action plan of digital health implementation for willing CAREC countries.

85. **Key challenges for innovations.** Even though innovative models were developed and implemented in some countries during the COVID-19 pandemic, other countries were missing sufficient technical capacity for adopting, implementing, and scaling up innovative models and solutions (footnote 36). Being able to rapidly adopt innovations is key to solving the current crisis and to preparing for future pandemics.

---

[76] ADB. 2022. *CAREC Digital Strategy 2030: Accelerating Digital Transformation for Regional Competitiveness and Inclusive Growth.* Manila.

86.   **Proposed actions.** The CAREC Health Strategy 2030 will focus on improving the technical capacity for adopting, implementing, scaling up, and sharing innovative models and solutions. Areas of intervention may include the following:

(i)   Creating awareness on existing national, regional, and global innovative solutions for mitigating health crises like the COVID-19 pandemic.
(ii)   Offering capacity-building workshops and webinars on innovative solutions in the health sector to CAREC member countries.
(iii) Exploring the development of a fund for supporting innovations in health emergencies.
(iv)   Supporting the creation of a regional innovations knowledge exchange platform to facilitate knowledge transfer and technical capacity building on health security.

5

IMPLEMENTATION MECHANISMS FOR CAREC HEALTH COOPERATION

A. Institutional Setup

87. For the CAREC countries to develop regional cooperation in health, an institutional structure must be established. The CAREC institutional structure will be taken as a starting point for aligning and incorporating the appropriate institutional arrangements for the CAREC Health Strategy (Figure 5). At the top, the CAREC Ministerial Conference functions as the main high-level policy and decision-making body, responsible for providing strategic guidance on issues of regional relevance and accountable for the overall results of the CAREC program. The Senior Officials' Meeting (SOM) monitors

progress on all operational clusters and sectors, recommends operational improvements, and ensures that the high-level decisions made at the CAREC Ministerial Conference are effectively implemented.

88. At the sector level, the overall CAREC health work will be led initially by the CAREC WGH.[77] This group is composed of high-level representatives from health-related government agencies with multidisciplinary expertise in various sectors, including agriculture and the environment. They have been appointed by their respective CAREC member countries since March 2021. The WGH would also include development partner

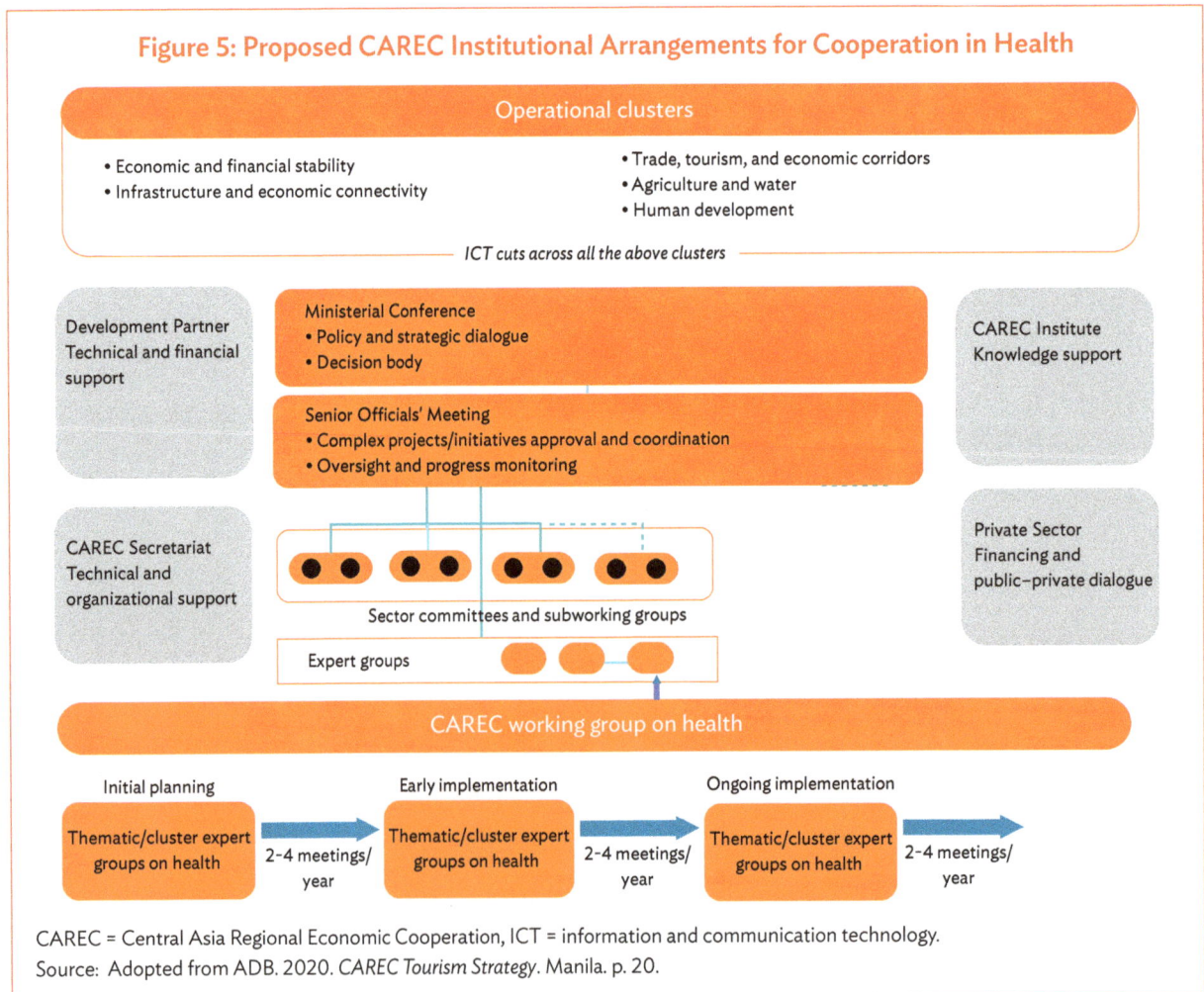

Figure 5: Proposed CAREC Institutional Arrangements for Cooperation in Health

CAREC = Central Asia Regional Economic Cooperation, ICT = information and communication technology.
Source: Adopted from ADB. 2020. *CAREC Tourism Strategy*. Manila. p. 20.

---

[77] Depending on the pace and scale of the progress made by the working group, it can later evolve into a full-fledged sector committee, like in more advanced CAREC sectors of transport and energy.

representatives, including WHO representatives, upon their willingness and availability. The CAREC Secretariat is responsible for providing technical, administrative, and organizational support during implementation of the CAREC Health Strategy 2030.

89.   The WGH will be tasked to (i) support the development and implementation of the CAREC Health Strategy 2030 and the Regional Investment Framework, identify and mobilize additional resources from other development partners for proposed regional investments in health, and lead the planning and delivery of health cooperation projects and activities at the country level; (ii) assure adequate engagement of and coordination with regional actors such as other operational clusters and sector committees and/or working groups, other regional networks and groupings, and academic and educational institutions; and (iii) contribute to the development and implementation of a supportive environment for regional health cooperation, taking into account gender equality issues through linkages, as needed, with the CAREC Regional Gender Expert Group.

90.   The WGH will be chaired by CAREC countries on a rotational basis following the CAREC chairmanship rules. The WGH, with support from the CAREC Secretariat, will be accountable to the CAREC SOM for delivering on the assigned tasks. It will also be responsible for regional action planning and development of health pipeline projects for inclusion in the Regional Investment Framework 2022–2026. In addition, the WGH will develop a rolling biennial work plan for each strategic pillar that will detail output-based and time-bound actions toward agreed milestones. Outputs may include research, knowledge products, capacity-building activities or policy-related actions, or other deliverables defined in the rolling work plan.

91.   There will be regular reporting of implementation progress against the work plan. Results will guide forward planning and milestone review, as well as provide lessons for adjusting activities and implementation mechanisms. This process of reflection and review ensures flexibility during strategy implementation to respond to the evolving programming context. The WGH, through the CAREC Secretariat, will track and compile results for reporting within the CAREC program. The WGH will be supported at the country level by the focal point—WGH Country Focal—nominated by each CAREC country, who will serve as the contact point for the CAREC Secretariat and the focal point for in-country liaison with the health ministry and related non-health agencies and sectors.

92.   The institutional mechanism of the CAREC program serves to facilitate and strengthen CAREC health cooperation within and beyond the health sector. Horizontal linkages between the CAREC WGH and other sector working groups and/or committees will be formed through a variety of means, including the participation of non-health sector stakeholders in WGH meetings, convening of cross-sector thematic discussions, and engagement of non-health stakeholders in project fact-finding and project preparation missions.

93.   Vertical linkages between the WGH and the CAREC SOM and CAREC Ministerial Meeting provide a mechanism to elevate the profile of health cooperation within the CAREC program. Following the practices of other CAREC sectors, the opportunity to convene meetings of CAREC health ministers as appropriate on a consensus basis will be explored as a mechanism to support high-level policy dialogue and decision making on issues critical to health cooperation in the region. The CAREC Institute will support the implementation of the CAREC Health Strategy 2030 through providing knowledge and technical analysis, including knowledge sharing among CAREC countries, as well as with developing member countries in other regions.

94.   Collaboration with the Regional Expert Working Group on gender issues according to the identified CAREC Gender Strategy health-related issues will be sought. These include strengthening surveillance systems across borders to control communicable and noncommunicable diseases

and improving access of women and men to quality medicines at more affordable costs across the region. In addition, there can be exploration and knowledge sharing on new technologies and digital solutions such as cross-border telehealth and e-health services. This will enhance access to health services, particularly of women, who have constrained mobility.

B. Cooperation and Partnerships

95. **Stakeholder engagement** will be critical in enabling strategy implementation and providing technical expertise and financing. In particular, the cooperation and support of those active in the fields of regional cooperation in health will be sought. In each of the countries, such stakeholders will likely include UN agencies, international finance institutions, bilateral development agencies, other development partners, civil society and community-based organizations, youth-led organizations, and academic institutions. In the CAREC region, those most likely to be involved include WHO; UNICEF; the CDC; Global Fund to fight AIDS, TB and Malaria; the World Bank; ADB; China International Development Agency; and the United States Agency for International Development (USAID).

96. Regional collaboration needs to be built on synergies among such agencies and existing initiatives through regular exchange of information and developing collaborative partnership frameworks to combine knowledge, skills, and capabilities and explore new funding mechanisms. In addition, mechanisms for developing partnerships with private entities in key areas such as public–private partnerships and insurance, data collection and statistics, surveillance, clinical and management, education, and skills development will be explored. Different approaches will be needed for cooperating with different groups of partners. For example, development partners who may be involved in several existing activities or who may have a mutual interest in promoting regional cooperation on relevant health security topics can become partners in regional cooperation projects and capacity development initiatives. Collaboration

with intergovernmental organizations may be sought through improved knowledge sharing and dialogue. Existing regional health initiatives could be expanded to include more CAREC countries or used as a framework for health cooperation (e.g., ABEC, Field Epidemiology Training Program). Cooperation with local governments in border areas will be sought as appropriate and where they carry out important public health functions. Where possible, cooperation with community-based organizations shall be explored to implement activities in border areas.

97. **Political commitment and policy dialogue.** Understanding and agreement facilitated by health policy dialogue and coordination among CAREC countries will be required to guide and lead the implementation of the CAREC Health Strategy 2030. This may involve close coordination and communication between countries at several levels, including developing agreements and facilitating relevant data sharing, and joint mechanisms for capacity building. Linked to this is the need for clear governance and leadership with efficiently functioning organizational structures. Creating a virtual knowledge platform for CAREC countries may be relevant for sharing ideas and enabling health cooperation.

98. According to the national assessments carried out, the common national institutions responsible for regional cooperation in the health sector may include ministries of health, the health committee of the Parliament, the President's office, the Prime Minister's office, and ministries of foreign affairs. They support implementation of the respective policies and programs at operational level through such agencies as departments of international cooperation, National Food Safety Agency, and Sanitary and Epidemiological Control Committee (Appendix 1).

99. **Multisector cooperation** at the national and local levels is needed since healthcare, as evidenced by the current COVID-19 pandemic, requires action by several sectors, including trade, tourism, environment, agriculture, customs control, and labor migration. This is particularly true for the

CAREC group of countries, for whom there are shared borders through which the spread of disease requires collaborative measures.

100. **Geographic clusters** shall be encouraged to address health security issues among the CAREC countries where there are shared borders, political-cultural affiliations, and common interests. Geographic country clusters can effectively facilitate activities and implement agreements between certain countries. Based on immediate geographic proximity and shared borders, and on existing health-related alliances and agreements, the proposed clusters are selectively detailed in Box 6.

C. Capacity Support

101. Through the CAREC health initiative, ideas will be generated for training and knowledge-sharing activities. Potential study tours or simulation exercises may enhance the capacity of relevant leaders and promoters of the CAREC health initiative. One approach to be considered for regional health capacity building is to explore strategic regional partnerships, either within CAREC or outside the region, such as with China CDC and the China National Health Development Research Center in the PRC, the Robert Koch Institute in Germany, or the Center for Global

---

Box 6: Selected Proposed Geographic Clusters

(i)   Azerbaijan, Georgia, and Kazakhstan (Azerbaijan and Georgia share common borders and may cooperate in the Lugar Center; all three cooperate in One Health—participating in the Electronic Integrated Disease Surveillance System).[a]

(ii)   The Kyrgyz Republic, Tajikistan, Turkmenistan, and Uzbekistan share extensive common borders, language, culture, socioeconomic factors, and bilateral agreements related to cross-border tuberculosis prevention and control to facilitate surveillance and referral of infectious diseases.[b]

(iii)   Mongolia and the People's Republic of China (PRC) share a common border; participate in similar projects on aligning food safety, animal health, and plant health with the World Trade Organization's SPS Agreement; and have similar infectious disease surveillance and investigative response initiatives.[c]

(iv)   The PRC and Pakistan share vaccine-related activities. The National Institute of Health of Pakistan cooperates with CanSinoBio (a vaccine developer based in the PRC) and with the Beijing Institute of Biotechnology.[d]

(v)   Azerbaijan, Kazakhstan, the Kyrgyz Republic, Tajikistan, Turkmenistan, and Uzbekistan developed ideas for joint actions under the United Nations Special Programme for the Economies of Central Asia.[e]

(vi)   Kazakhstan, the Kyrgyz Republic, Tajikistan, Turkmenistan, and Uzbekistan joined the Central Asian Leadership Program of education for sustainable development.[f]

(vii)   Countries along economic corridors such as the Almaty–Bishkek Economic Corridor.

[a]   A. Burdakov, A. Ukharov, and T.G. Wahl. 2013. One Health Surveillance with Electronic Integrated Disease Surveillance System. *Online Journal of Public Health Information*. 5 (1). p. e199.

[b]   *Stop TB Partnership*. Press Release. 2017. Central Asia Addresses Cross-Border Tuberculosis Prevention and Control Among Migrants.

[c]   ADB. 2015. *Henan Sustainable Livestock Farming and Product Safety Demonstration Project*. Manila; ADB. 2015. *Regional Upgrades of Sanitary and Phytosanitary Measures for Trade Project*. Manila.

[d]   *Reuters*. 2021. Pakistan Produces Chinese CanSinoBio COVID Vaccine, Brands it PakVak.

[e]   United Nations Economic Commission for Europe (UNECE). n.d. United Nations Special Programme for the Economies of Central Asia (SPECA).

[f]   Regional Environmental Centre for Central Asia. 2021. The Central Asian Leadership Program of Education for Sustainable Development (Calpesd).

Source: Asian Development Bank.

Health at the Graduate Institute of International and Development Studies in Switzerland. These institutions have expertise in health security, health diplomacy, and other areas that can support the implementation of regional health cooperation. In addition, the role of the CAREC Institute in facilitating capacity development and coordination in the health sector could be further explored.

102. Twinning for experience and procedural how-to-do skills sharing is another approach worth exploring. This could include both institutional twinning and professional twinning between specialists from CAREC countries—with input of international "twin" specialists from other countries. Such twinning can be applied through technical assistance to various CAREC regional or country-centered efforts to build capacity. This could involve (i) a technical assistance for experience exchange in adapting clinical practice guidelines to current antibiotic resistance situations; (ii) twinning, networking and exchange for lab specialists or (iii) twinning among decision makers in skills and methods to interpret epidemiological data for guiding pandemic containment measures.

103. Research and knowledge products can be developed to help ensure that health activities are feasible and sustainable. There should be an emphasis on basing future projects around regional cooperation on the best available evidence. Knowledge products may serve to build capacity in CAREC countries in appropriate topics and fields of interest to countries.

D. Regional Investment Framework

104. To support the implementation of the CAREC Health Strategy 2030, a regional investment framework for 2022–2026 will be developed to guide partner investments and meet the gap in effectively addressing key regional needs, including protecting vulnerable populations in border areas. The investment framework will serve as a tool for prioritizing projects and will allow for greater coordination among development partners and mobilization of resources. The investments

shall cover regional projects and initiatives under the four strategic pillars. It will detail relevant project proposals and outline the investment case of each. The framework will include potential public–private partnerships, if appropriate, with indicative budgets, cost–benefit analyses, and recommendations for including gender-sensitive elements.

105. In recognition of the varying levels of development and capacity of CAREC countries, flexibility will be needed in allowing two or more countries to implement regional projects and initiatives. CAREC health cooperation projects will form an integral part of the Regional Investment Framework, 2022–2026. Projects included in this framework will align with the CAREC Health Strategy priorities and address criteria for regionality, that is, projects that contribute to CAREC health cooperation outcomes through either

(i)   a joint initiative (cluster) of two or more CAREC countries, or
(ii) a single country initiative that has a clear impact on other CAREC countries.

106. The investment framework will be updated on a regular basis to guide programming and mobilize development partner resources. The Regional Investment Framework, 2022–2026 will include initiatives financed by ADB, CAREC governments, other development partners, and initiatives for which a financing source will be identified.

6

MONITORING OUTCOMES OF THE CAREC HEALTH STRATEGY

107. The CAREC WGH will be responsible for monitoring the implementation of the health strategy and investment framework on an annual basis and for proposing adjustments, as needed, based on countries' emerging needs and priorities. The monitoring framework for CAREC health cooperation is shown in Table 4. The framework sets out select indicators under each of the strategy's four pillars and crosscutting themes that capture key achievements of CAREC health cooperation. Several SDG indicators are included in the framework, linking the strategy to higher-level outcomes. Improvements in these SDG-linked indicators are only likely to be apparent over the medium to long term, and are not attributable solely to the CAREC Health Strategy programming.

108. An operational results framework will be developed in more detail and will further specify the output- and outcome-level indicators contained in the summary results framework. This will provide a more specific measure of accomplishments that are directly attributable to CAREC health cooperation projects and activities. The results framework is aligned with the health sector outputs and outcomes contained in the wider CAREC Program Results Framework. In this way, monitoring outcomes of CAREC health cooperation will inform progress toward the CAREC program's overall results framework.[78]

Table 4: CAREC Health Strategy Results Framework

Goal		Indicators	Baseline	Source
Enhanced regional health security		By 2030: Incidence of EIDs among population Average IHR score of CAREC countries Number of CAREC countries that incorporate joint regional approaches and cross-sector activities in their UHC and/or health sector strategies or plans[a]	Total CAREC COVID-19 cases in 2021 TBD	CAREC countries and Secretariat National health strategies/ plans CAREC reports
Strategic Pillar	**Outcome**	**Indicators**	**Baseline**	**Source**
1. Leadership and human resource capacity	Strengthened regional leadership, coordination, and workforce	Coordination and governance: Intersectoral Support Framework is established Number of joint country activities conducted under the CAREC Health Strategy	0 0	CAREC Secretariat CAREC Secretariat
		Workforce skills and capacity: Number of health-related personnel (sex-disaggregated) trained through CAREC support to address issues related to health security[a]	TBD	CAREC countries and Secretariat
Strategic Pillar	**Outcome**	**Indicators**	**Baseline**	**Source**
2. Technical preparedness	Improved surveillance and laboratory infrastructure	Surveillance response: Number of CAREC countries using harmonized surveillance data and common analysis criteria	TBD	CAREC countries and Secretariat

continued on next page

---

[78] CAREC. 2020. *Program Results Framework.*

Table 4 continued

Strategic Pillar	Outcome	Indicators	Baseline	Source
		Laboratory infrastructure: Number of CAREC countries with diagnostic laboratories that have recognized capacity for providing high-quality PCR analysis	TBD	CAREC countries and Secretariat
Strategic Pillar	**Outcome**	**Indicators**	**Baseline**	**Source**
3. Access to supplies and surge capacity	Increased capacity to access supplies and meet surge demands	Regulatory mechanisms: Regional cooperation mechanism established to strengthen regulatory capacity	0	CAREC Secretariat
		Procurement mechanisms: Number of regional procurement mechanisms developed (from information sharing to actual procurement)	0	CAREC countries and Secretariat
		Supply chain management: Regional Supply Chain Risk Management Plan developed	0	CAREC countries and Secretariat
Strategic Pillar	**Outcome**	**Indicators**	**Baseline**	**Source**
4. Vulnerable population groups and border health	Enhanced health services for migrant groups, border communities, and vulnerable groups	Access: Research conducted on the needs of CAREC cross-border communities and mobile populations, including women and vulnerable groups	0	CAREC countries and Secretariat
		Burden of disease: Number of regional collaboration initiatives for cross-border support to migrants with chronic infectious diseases (e.g., TB, HIV)	TBD	CAREC countries and Secretariat
	Outcomes	**Indicators**	**Baseline**	**Source**
Crosscutting themes	Sufficient health information systems, data management, regional knowledge sharing, and innovation capacity	Digital health/innovation: Number of nationally agreed vision and road maps for the interoperability of information systems	TBD	CAREC countries and Secretariat
	Disaggregation of data by gender assured; specific needs of women considered in health planning and design of services and infrastructure	Gender: Number of CAREC countries with capacity to collect sex-disaggregated routine surveillance data on EIDs Research conducted on the sex-differentiated effects of the outbreaks and pandemics, especially on female health workers, female patients, and on households with female heads	TBD 0	CAREC countries and Secretariat CAREC countries and Secretariat
	Outcome	**Indicator**	**Baseline**	**Source**
Institutions and governance	Institutional platform for regional health cooperation established[a]	Number of joint regional health solutions developed under CAREC[a]	0	CAREC Secretariat

CAREC = Central Asia Regional Economic Cooperation Program, COVID-19 = coronavirus disease, EID = emerging infectious disease, IHR = International Health Regulations, PCR = polymerase chain reaction, TB = tuberculosis, TBD = to be determined, UHC = universal health coverage.

[a] Aligned with CAREC Program Results Framework.

Source: ADB.

APPENDIX 1
STRATEGIC PILLARS AND DETAILS OF OBJECTIVES

A. Pillar 1: Leadership and Human Resource Capacity

Strategic Objective 1.1—Coordination and governance. Improved interministerial and multisector policy coordination, international support, and health system governance capacity in the Central Asia Regional Economic Cooperation (CAREC) region to respond to epidemic and pandemic health threats.

Key Actions

(i) Improve interministerial and intersectoral coordination and governance in the CAREC region, including regional dialogue mechanisms; mapping of status quo of International Health Regulations (IHR); and knowledge and experience sharing among countries in the CAREC region, according to information currently available.

(ii) Establish and strengthen emergency operating centers (EOCs), in close collaboration with IHR focal points, in member countries and provide a central location from which to coordinate data collection and response to public health threats at the national level and support exchange and networking among regional EOCs to strengthen more coordinated response.[1]

(iii) Strengthen joint outbreak response among CAREC countries and support them to carry out health emergency drills and cooperation.

(iv) Further explore options and possible piloting to implement pandemic risk financing.

Other aspects for potential cooperation and improvement:

(i) Develop an Intersectoral Support Framework to ensure a coordinated approach to managing public health emergencies across partners and sectors.

(ii) Undertake information sharing and capacity building, such as on outbreak preparation (workshops, regional training programs).

(iii) Explore establishing regional dialogue and approaches to support dynamic and effective coordination efforts.

(iv) Continuing study of reemerging infectious diseases.

---

[1] Center for Strategic & International Studies. n.d. Polio Emergency Operations Centers (accessed July 2021).

Strategic Objective 1.2—Workforce skills and capacity. Sufficient workforce skills and capacity—especially in public health emergency leadership, public health, epidemiology, and research—for planning and implementing effective measures and innovations in response to public health threats, including the coronavirus disease (COVID-19) pandemic.

Key Actions

(i)   Strengthen the technical capacity of policymakers, public health managers, and planners, as well as epidemiologists and data scientists, in health policy, planning, management, and implementation of effective and gender-sensitive measures to respond to public health threats and emergencies, including the COVID-19 pandemic; enhance resilience and pandemic preparedness through regional capacity building and knowledge-sharing opportunities and platforms; and improve the leadership and governance skills of health policymakers on health emergencies.

(ii) Strengthen knowledge and skills of the public health and epidemiological workforce (male and female), including mid-level health professionals (e.g., lab technicians) through regional webinars; and recommend skills-focused, continuous medical training modules on laboratory operations and methods, laboratory quality assurance and quality control, laboratory biosafety, and evidence base for epidemic countermeasures to control and contain key regional health threats.

(iii) Improve the distribution of health workforce in CAREC countries (e.g., by preparing capacity development plans for rural areas).

(iv) Improve technical skills for early warning, alert, and response in emergencies; support CAREC member countries in the development of field-based tools (e.g., online, desktop, and mobile application that can be rapidly configured and deployed); and conduct training programs that include female participants.

(v)   Improve research and appropriate best practice results on communicable and noncommunicable diseases (NCDs), especially from within the region, promoted through relevant regional research training opportunities, study reports, and webinars, provided by regional and international agencies.

Other aspects for potential cooperation and improvement:

(i)   Explore potential joint regional capacity building efforts in key NCD topics (e.g., the regional challenge of rising cerebrovascular stroke deaths due to hypertension and diabetes, and other NCD priority areas).

(ii) Explore developing recommendations for the region based on what has proven to reduce risk for NCDs elsewhere in the world (e.g., cerebrovascular disease morbidity and mortality).

(iii) Support regional and country-specific formative research on knowledge, attitudes, and practices related to healthcare service demand, infectious disease prevention, vaccines, and other regional health issues.

(iv) Explore the possibility of establishing regional mechanisms for identification and funding of research and development activities in healthcare. The relevant and high-priority areas may include Multidrug-Resistant Tuberculosis and expansion of research programs with the involvement of Centers for Disease Control and Prevention regional offices, the Structured Operational Research and Training IniTiative (SORT IT), and the Asian Development Bank (ADB)-Japan Scholarship Program.

(v)   Improve capacity to implement, monitor, and evaluate new or innovative products and approaches.

(vi) Support regional meetings of epidemiologists, infectious disease doctors, and representatives of the scientific community. The regional meetings will serve as a venue for constant exchange of knowledge, experience, and skills on innovative solutions to fight infections; technological developments; and sharing of results achieved.

(vii) Explore the possibility of establishing grant financing mechanisms for joint studies addressing population health needs in the region (e.g., health inequalities and development of regional health inequality standard indicators, poverty-related disease, barriers to COVID-19 vaccination, and health needs of most vulnerable population groups).

(viii)   Establish a roster of national and/or regional experts by respective technical areas.

(ix)   Offer capacity training workshops and seminars to public health clinical and nonclinical workforce—either virtually or on the ground—to further expand their knowledge on public health crisis situations;[2] and build on the successful experience of the Centers for Disease Control and Prevention (CDC)-supported Field Epidemiology and Laboratory Training Programs in the region (e.g., the South Caucasus),[3] which are designed to be adaptable to the needs of any given country in the region, where many fundamental similarities in the skills and knowledge required by public health workers exist.

(x)   Support countries in harmonizing their policies and strategies for medical education/training/curriculum, licensing, and registration; and in harmonizing policies and strategies for procurement and supply chain education and training.

(xi)   Strengthen capacity on health impact assessments (HIA) through multisector approach.

(xii)   Support willing CAREC member countries in exchanging information on residency training programs in select priority areas such as infectious diseases and family medicine.[4]

(xiii)   Support willing CAREC member countries in improving the quality of medical education at all levels, including postgraduate medical education and continuous professional development.

(xiv)   Support the development of generic online tools for implementing training programs that can be used for all fields and specialties of medicine and public health.

(xv)   Support human resources for health planning to ensure preparedness in responding to various public health threats; enhance surge capacity; and ensure a sufficient supply and deployment of health workers, including across borders.

Ideas Provider: Ideas on preparedness and resilience of health workforce might be found in the special issue on healthcare workforce around the globe in the *International Journal on Health Planning and Management*.[5]

B.   Pillar 2: Technical Preparedness

Strategic Objective 2.1—Surveillance response. Effective surveillance response to public health threats, including the COVID-19 pandemic (e.g., improve surveillance systems, explore regional dashboards with automated early warning systems, and compile regionally aligned awareness-raising materials on communicable diseases.

Key Actions

(i)   Improve the sharing of epidemic information according to IHR and in line with laws and regulations in the respective CAREC member countries.

(ii)   Exchange strategies of sampling to enable cross-country comparisons, improve capacity for referral transport of specimens, and reduce turnaround time from sampling to result report; and boost capacity for sensitivity and reliability through quality assurance and upgraded biosafety standards.

---

[2]   Some CAREC countries have implemented the Field Epidemiology Training Program (Box 5, ii).

[3]   TEPHINET. South Caucasus Field Epidemiology and Laboratory Training Program.

[4]   Suggestions on how to support rapid learning for healthcare workers could be found here: B. Engelbrecht et al. 2021. Prioritizing People and Rapid Learning in Times of Crisis: A Virtual Learning Initiative to Support Health Workers during the COVID-19 Pandemic. *Int J Health Plann Manage.* 36 (S1). pp. 168–173.

[5]   E. Kuhlmann, G. Dussault, and T. Correia. 2021. Special Issue: Global Health and Health Workforce Development: Education, Management and Policy during the COVID-19 Crisis and Beyond. *Int J of Health Planning and Management.* 36 (S1). pp. 1–203.

Other aspects for potential cooperation and improvement:

(i)   Establish regional dialogue as a sharing platform for shared approaches to surveillance sampling and testing, including promotion of sentinel surveillance, to allow cross-country comparative and compatible COVID-19 statistics.
(ii)   Help in sharing electronic surveillance data among willing countries in the region (including standardization of data across countries, as well as region-wide access to electronic early warning, surveillance, and risk communication systems).
(iii)   Help implement standardized surveillance systems, including One Health, in willing CAREC countries.
(iv)   Provide technical support to member countries to strengthen early warning, alert, and response in emergencies, through training and development of field-based tools (e.g., online, desktop, and mobile applications that can be rapidly configured and deployed).
(v)   Explore establishing regional dashboards that provide an automated early warning system for epidemiologists in the public health sector in willing CAREC member countries. The system can generate signals or alerts when they detect a possible infectious disease outbreak among humans and animals, including antimicrobial resistance (One Health). During emergencies, existing national public health surveillance systems may be underperforming, disrupted, or nonexistent; they may quickly become overwhelmed. Thus, it is crucial to immediately establish an early warning system to detect and react rapidly to suspected disease outbreaks.[6]
(vi)   Support the establishment of EOCs so that they can coordinate all components of health security responses.
(vii)   Support the effective integration of the newly established EOCs into the existing regional coordination mechanisms and platforms (e.g., through WHO regional offices and UN Development Coordination Office Regional Directors); assess the implementation and operational gaps of these mechanisms; and provide technical and programmatic support as needed.
(viii) Support the development of a regional handbook for awareness on communicable disease and pandemic control, including risk communication and vaccines, among others.
(ix)   Support the regional capacity development in social behavior change communications and risk communication and community engagement in willing CAREC countries.

Ideas Provider: EOC alert system, Pakistan-EOC.

Building on: Regional Inception Workshop suggestions, cluster meetings, national assessments.

Strategic Objective 2.2—Laboratory infrastructure. Sufficient laboratory infrastructure and management in compliance with international quality and biosafety requirements.

Key Actions

(i)   Strengthen national and regional laboratory networks and laboratory systems for testing,[7] as well as multifunctional equipment and methods for detecting potential pathogens (e.g., boosting polymerase chain reaction (PCR) capacity and next-generation sequencing capacity, and exploring the establishment of the Central Asian Regional Centre for Epidemiology, Virology and Bacteriology.[8]

---

[6]   World Health Organization. 2019. *Public Health Situation Analysis.* Presentation for Health Cluster Coordination Training. Brazzaville, Republic of the Congo. May.
[7]   A network is the physical number of laboratories and their served catchment areas, served facilities, or served populations. Laboratory systems include functionalities of reporting, quality assurance, and quality control mechanisms.
[8]   *Turkmenistan Golden Age News.* 2021. Central Asian Regional Center for Epidemiology, Virology and Bacteriology.

(ii)   Improve laboratory infrastructure and ensure proper laboratory workflow and management according to international quality and biosafety requirements, including through existing regional initiatives and hubs.

(iii) Implement support quality management systems in laboratories through mentoring by trained national mentors.

Other aspects for potential cooperation and improvement:

(i)   Provide technical support in the assessment and establishment of testing capacity for novel emerging pathogens, including planning for surge capacity, by establishing decentralized testing capacity in subnational laboratories under the supervision of the national reference laboratory.

(ii)   Explore options to engage private laboratory services or the academic sector to address gaps, such as limited testing facilities, by giving timely access to testing for people living in remote and border areas through using mobile laboratories, as well as point-of-care lab equipment.

(iii) Support development and implementation of regional quality assurance and control mechanisms, including implementation of laboratory quality management standards (LQMS) (e.g., guidelines, standard operating procedures [SOPs]).

(iv)   Support LQMS strengthening through comprehensive assessments, strategic and operational planning, and supporting implementation (e.g., regional laboratory experts pool and regional training centers).

Ideas Provider: Results from the Almaty–Bishkek Economic Corridor (ABEC) reference lab project for the implementation of further reference labs within CAREC.[9]

C.   Pillar 3: Access to Supplies and Surge Capacity

Strategic Objective 3.1—Regulatory mechanisms. Effective regulatory mechanisms and standards for medications and supplies.

Key Actions

(i)   Improve regulatory mechanisms, standards, and procedures for medicines, laboratory equipment, and supplies by harmonizing policies and regulations for authorization, registration, and importation of products and investing in regional cooperation mechanisms to strengthen regulatory capacity.

(ii)   Create more competitive and efficient market mechanisms to increase supply and reduce prices for medicines and supplies.

(iii) Improve visibility and management of end-to-end procurement and supply chain from manufacturer through consumption (i.e., regional coordination of procurement and supply chain management activities, alignment and harmonization of data standards, and sharing of information and insights).

(iv)   Streamline the movement of medical goods in the region by harmonizing the import and export of medicines and supplies, and standardizing and sharing product master data, supply base, and contracting processes.

---

[9]   ADB. 2018. *Assessment Report for Diagnostic and Reference Laboratory Functions in National Laboratory Systems in Kazakhstan and the Kyrgyz Republic*. Manila.

Other aspects for potential cooperation and improvement:

(i)   Adopt standards (e.g., Global Traceability Standard and Product Catalogs) to enable regional product verification and traceability and reduce the risk of procuring poor-quality products.

Strategic Objective 3.2—Procurement mechanisms. Efficient national and regional procurement mechanisms for medications and supplies.

Key Actions

(i)   Develop procurement and supply management capacity among health policymakers and personnel in the health sector and align approach, training, and tools across the region.
(ii)   Improve procurement activities (e.g., procurement policies and procedures, standardization of supplier base, contracting, and supplier performance management).
(iii)   Further develop options for regional manufacturing and stockpiles.

Other potential aspects for cooperation and improvement:

(i)   Set up regional coordination mechanisms to share information, best practices, and tools and convene discussions on procurement and supply chain management.
(ii)   Improve procurement and supply chain policies and procedures to support more competitive markets, with consideration for adoption of procurement marketplaces and international procurement agents.
(iii)   Digitize procurement and supply chain activities to provide end-to-end visibility, enabling more effective real-time decision making.
(iv)   Explore the establishment of a regional procurement mechanism that can provide market visibility, secure supply, negotiate good prices, and guarantee quality (i.e., opt-in emergency procurement).
(v)   Support the development of emergency-use procurement policies to enable quicker access to medicines and supplies (i.e., novel Dx, Vx).
(vi)   Simplify procedures and remove barriers for customs clearance and importing and exporting of health products between countries in the region.
(vii)   Start longer-term planning for resource pooling to build regional manufacturing capacity (e.g., personal protective equipment [PPE], diagnostics, oxygen, ventilators, labs, tests, drugs, and vaccines).

Strategic Objective 3.3—Supply chain management. Reliable supply chain management that assures sufficient supply and stocks for emergency situations.

Key Actions

(i)   Improve supply and stocks for emergency situations, including the use of virtual control rooms (e.g., situation rooms), and joint opt-in procurement mechanisms.
(ii)   Develop a supply chain risk management plan.

Other aspects for potential cooperation and improvement:

(i)   Establish a regional virtual situation room to provide visibility of procurement and supply chain, enable real-time decision making, and ensure that supplies can meet the demand.
(ii)   Explore and assess vulnerabilities across the medical supplies supply chain from raw material availability, storage, and transport to policies and regulations and human resources.

D. Pillar 4: Vulnerable Population Groups and Border Health

Strategic Objective 4.1—Access. Improved access to health services and cross-border referrals.

Key Actions

(i) Research on health needs of CAREC cross-border communities and mobile populations, including women and other vulnerable groups.
(ii) Improve accessibility of health services while avoiding financial hardship and providing referral options to enhance continuity of care, especially on primary health care (PHC), for labor migrants and mobile populations crossing borders in high numbers, with special consideration of women's health needs.
(iii) Define a minimum package of actions in response to public health threats in border areas and/or points of entry, including (a) access to medical services, including diagnostic services; (b) access to equipment and personnel for transporting infected travelers to an appropriate medical facility; (c) surveillance activities; (d) risk communication and social mobilization; (e) environmental health (i.e., vector control, solid and liquid waste management, potable water, and general sanitation); and (f) data management and information exchange in close collaboration with WHO.
(iv) Strengthen or expand agreements that target portability of benefits for migrants.
(v) Improve the infrastructure and technical capacity of testing and quarantine facilities in border areas and points of entry, including for COVID-19 patients, to protect travelers and the population.
(vi) Support the upgrading of health facility infrastructure in border areas and cross-border economic corridors.

Other aspects for potential cooperation and improvement:

(i) Promote a regional multisector approach for working with migrants (i.e., customs, police services, health, and social services).
(ii) Improve data on specific health needs of mobile populations through formative research.
(iii) Improve gender-sensitive Risk Communication and Community Engagement (RCCE) strategies to target and reach migrants, mobile populations, and border communities effectively.[10]

Ideas Provider/Building on: Regional Inception Workshop suggestions; scoping study; Thailand's migrants' health insurance scheme; regional mechanism for linking registration of documented migrants to social security services, possibly building on the Commonwealth of Independent States (CIS) electronic card for migrants;[11] how regular immigrants and stateless persons in the territory of the Republic of Kazakhstan have the right to free medical assistance; and cluster meetings.

Strategic Objective 4.2 —Burden of disease. Decreased burden of communicable diseases among migrants, border communities, and vulnerable population groups.

---

[10] ADB. Guidelines for Regional Communication and Community Engagement (RCCE) Utilizing Social and Behavior Change (SBC) for COVID-19 Communication. Unpublished.
[11] CAREC members of the CIS include Azerbaijan, Kazakhstan, the Kyrgyz Republic, Tajikistan, and Uzbekistan. See ADB. 2021. *Toward CAREC 2030: Enhancing Regional Cooperation in the Health Sector—A Scoping Study*. Manila.

Key Actions

(i)   Improve quality of treatment for migrants with tuberculosis (TB) and HIV (e.g., explore to expand existing agreements on the eligibility of migrants for HIV and TB diagnosis, care, and treatment in willing CAREC countries).

Other aspects for potential cooperation and improvement:

(i)   Support the design and implementation of cross-border mobile health services.
(ii)   Support the provision of mobile ambulances in border areas to broaden services for migrants.
(iii)   Support the provision of basic medical items for migrants crossing borders.
(iv)   Provide transport means for mobile populations to healthcare facilities.
(v)   Strengthen regional mechanisms for addressing highly prevalent infectious diseases like TB and HIV.
(vi)   Implement a regional collaboration for transborder regional projects to support migrants with chronic diseases such as HIV, TB, and malaria.[12]
(vii)   Improve access to good-quality TB drugs, as well as adequate access to transborder health services, and ensure quality of care for patients with these diseases.
(viii)   Explore an electronic medical passport or record to ensure the continuity of care in willing CAREC countries.
(ix)   Explore the establishment of a regional institute to facilitate regional cross-border collaboration on zoonoses (following the One Health approach), as well as TB and HIV in the long run. This institute could also serve as a knowledge-sharing platform for the region.

Ideas Provider/Building on: Regional Inception Workshop suggestions; scoping study.

Strategic Objective 4.3—Infection prevention and control (IPC). Effective infection prevention and control measures in border regions to protect travelers and the population, including for COVID-19 cases.

Key Actions

(i)   Improve IPC measures, including in hospitals and primary care facilities in border areas, such as evidence-based, facility-adapted IPC guidelines and SOPs.

Other aspects for potential cooperation and improvement:

(i)   Establish a follow-up system for patients crossing borders with infectious diseases that ensures continuity of treatment for migrants and border-crossing communities with communicable diseases.

---

[12]   The regional collaboration could build on the already existing collaboration between Kazakhstan, the Kyrgyz Republic, and Tajikistan. They signed agreements on cross-border cooperation for TB and MDR-TB control, prevention, and care among migrant workers from Central Asia and on the establishment of a mechanism for exchanging information on TB patients among countries through the Euro WHO TB electronic platform (tbconsilium.org). These agreements were approved as a result of a 3-year program initiated in Kazakhstan in late 2014 with support from the Global Fund to Fight AIDS, Tuberculosis, and Malaria (the Global Fund); Project HOPE; WHO; International Organization for Migration (IOM); the Joint United Nations Programme on HIV/AIDS; and the International Federation of Red Cross and Red Crescent Societies. The program is aligned with WHO recommendations for cross-border TB control in Europe and Kazakhstan's national plan to combat TB. A potential entry point for further regional cooperation and integration in this area under CAREC is to deepen the regional dialogue and expand these agreements to engage more countries. See ADB. 2021. *Toward CAREC 2030: Enhancing Regional Cooperation in the Health Sector—A Scoping Study*. Manila.

E.   Crosscutting Issues

1.   Gender

Strategic Objective—Gender. Disaggregation of data by gender assured; specific needs of women considered in health planning and design of services and infrastructure.

Key Actions

(i)   Improve sex-disaggregation of data in the health sector of CAREC region through application of the CAREC Working Group on Health program.
(ii)   Inform about gender concepts, meanings, gaps, and implementation options in health projects.
(iii)   Include specific needs of women in health planning and designing of services.

Other aspects for potential cooperation and improvement:

(i)   Improve RCCE strategies to address women's needs effectively (footnote 10).

2.   Digital Health

Strategic Objective—Digital health. Sufficient health information systems, data management, and regional knowledge sharing.

Key Actions

(i)   Identify willing CAREC member countries' digital health priorities and assess their digital health landscapes as appropriate to suggest and support implementation of suitable digital health solutions.
(ii)   In partnership with willing CAREC member countries, conduct gaps assessment for achieving graded stepwise health system data interoperability. For example, identify gaps currently hampering the ability of different health sector information technology (IT) systems to "speak to each other," including among laboratory devices and applications (systems such as patient records and encounter registers), so that data can be accessed, exchanged, integrated, and cooperatively used in a coordinated manner within and across organizational, regional, and national boundaries to provide timely and seamless portability of information—optimizing health security.
(iii)   Based on the gap analysis, propose health data exchange architectures, application interfaces, and standards that enable data to be accessed and shared appropriately and securely across the complete spectrum of care in willing CAREC member countries, and provide the necessary training when such sharing is to take place within all applicable settings and with relevant stakeholders.
(iv)   Launch practical experimental initiatives for regionally unified coding of health data for willing CAREC countries through CAREC-wide promotion of WHO-recommended International Classification of Disease ICD-10 (and upcoming ICD-11) and International Classification of Primary Care to help ensure cross-country compatible and comparable data in national health IT systems and databases.
(v)   Engage in regional policy dialogues and knowledge exchange where information on successful digital approaches and policies to address challenges can be exchanged and fostered between countries.
(vi)   Promote and strengthen capacity on standardized and interoperable health information systems to overcome separate vertical systems and overlapping sources of data.
(vii)   Improve data management and data capture mechanisms, including quality of captured data capacity, analytical capacity, and presentation skills.
(viii)   Adopt methods to enable cross-border data sharing and use in willing CAREC member countries.

(ix) Strengthen digital leadership and digital skills among top-level decision makers.
(x)   Develop a sustainable and realistic regional action plan of digital health implementation for willing CAREC countries.

Other aspects for potential cooperation and improvement:

(i)   Support willing countries in assessing their level of digital readiness and maturity, which would contribute to the development of a national digital health strategy and an effective monitoring and evaluation plan that links stages of maturity with evaluation methods. The digital health strategy would reflect a country's health sector goals, the Sustainable Development Goals and Universal Health Coverage. This would encourage the adoption of an integrated health information system by identifying and addressing overlapping data sources and data sets; reducing data fragmentation; and supporting establishment of legislative, regulatory, and policy frameworks.

(ii) Promote best digital practices to enable top-level change management that will enable faster adoption of digital health into countries' health system landscapes. This will support and leverage the benefits of digital health practices at every level of the healthcare system. Digital health adoption and implementation should not be treated as a separate process, but rather a supportive method of addressing challenges in countries' health systems. Adopting a system of inculcating digital best practices into various levels of the healthcare system will aid in developing strategies and policies that can take advantage of a new window of opportunities. This will also enable domestic and/or regional environment for new business, investment, trade, and economic growth.

(iii) Support drafting a nationally agreed vision and road map for the interoperability of clinical data in both the public and private sector in willing CAREC countries. This will support the development and adoption of base-level requirements for using digital technology and support the collection of high-quality data through standardized clinical terminologies, a unique identifier, and data standards that ensure the secure exchange of health information.

(iv) Create a safe learning environment that supports the sharing of national digital health strategies, the impact of health service digitalization, digital challenges, and achievements. The CAREC platform could support facilitation of regional and/or national annual digital health workshops; forums on current digital tools, and published regional case studies that can be used to provide evidence on the performance of digital solutions to support health sector goals; and coordination with key stakeholders, including multilateral, bilateral, and technical agencies. This could provide opportunities for health innovation exchange where digital health policymakers, clinicians, researchers, and innovative start-up companies can collaborate to develop new digital health products and services. The CAREC platform could also support national digital health leadership by creating a peer-to-peer network of digital health champions to drive cultural change and awareness of digital health within the health sector.

(v)   Strengthen nongovernment, community, and workforce education providers in delivering training, resources, and curricula that support the health sector workforce and consumers in using digital technologies competently and confidently.[13]

(vi) Support the development of national digital health competencies, standards, and best practice guidelines in willing CAREC countries that promote digital health into national workforce accreditation and workplace practice. This would support the monitoring and evaluation of digital health practice, improve the capturing of high-quality data, and improve analytical capacity and data presentation skills.

(vii) Leverage existing coordination mechanisms among development partners to ensure ongoing commitment to country digital health priorities and avoid duplicating interventions.

---

[13] L.A. Long, G. Pariyo, and K. Kallander. 2018. Digital Technologies for Health Workforce Development in Low- and Middle-Income Countries: A Scoping Review. *Glob Health Sci. Pract.* 6 (S1). pp. S41–S48.

3. Innovations

Strategic Objective—Improved capacity to develop, implement, and utilize innovative solutions.

Key Actions

(i)   Create awareness on existing national, regional, and global innovative solutions for mitigating health crises like the COVID-19 pandemic.
(ii)   Offer capacity-building workshops and webinars on innovative solutions in the health sector to CAREC member countries.
(iii)   Explore the development of a fund for supporting innovations in emergencies.
(iv)   Support the creation of a regional innovations knowledge exchange platform to facilitate knowledge transfer and technical capacity building on health security.

Other aspects for potential cooperation and improvement:

(i)   Create opportunities to support innovative pioneering initiatives across the region among the private and public sector, governments, researchers, and providers by encouraging the selection, adaptation, testing, and piloting at-scale evidence-based digital applications, interventions, and digital services for care, information sharing across borders, and widening access to telehealth services throughout the region.
(ii)   Explore the possibility of building a fund supporting innovations in emergencies (e.g., seed money, hackathons).
(iii)   Support policies to enable private sector engagement in emergency situations.
(iv)   Support research in the form of clinical trials and field epidemiological trials to document efficacy of innovations and to provide an evidence base for which innovations are of value and safe.

Ideas Provider: ADB microsite on innovations around COVID-19.

Building on: CAREC website and/or focus on innovations around the health sector (compilation), cluster meetings, and feedback on innovation compilation.

APPENDIX 2
SUMMARY OF HEALTH SECTOR STRATEGIES

Country	Main National Health Sector Document(s)	Strategic Priorities
Afghanistan	National Health Strategy, 2016–2020	(i) Governance; (ii) institutional development; (iii) public health; (iv) health services; (v) human resources for health; and (vi) monitoring and evaluation, health information, learning, and knowledge and/or evidence-based practices.
Azerbaijan	Strategic Plan of the Ministry of Health, 2014–2020	(i) Increasing the percentage of gross domestic product dedicated to current health expenditure; (ii) developing mechanisms to ensure effective execution of the health budget; (iii) strengthening institutions in the health system for service delivery; (iv) increasing levels of devolution in the health system; (v) implementing preventive measures to tackle the burden of disease; (vi) launching a state program to improve child health; (vii) ensuring financial and physical access to vital medicines; and (viii) bolstering human resources for health.
China, People's Republic of	14th Five Year Plan for National Economic and Social Development and Long-Range Objectives for 2030	(i) Establish strong public health system, (ii) deepen reforms in health system, (iii) improve nationwide medical insurance system, (iv) traditional Chinese medicine promotion and innovation, (v) promote physical education, and (vi) carry out patriotic health campaigns.
	Thirteenth Five Year Plan for Health Sector, 2016–2020	(i) Disease prevention and treatment, as well as basic public healthcare services; (ii) maternal and infant health promotion; (iii) birth-defect prevention and treatment; (iv) community-level medical service provision strengthening; (v) traditional Chinese medicine promotion and innovation; (vi) smarter health care; (vii) fitness promotion on the population level; and (viii) food and medicine safety.
Georgia	Georgian Health Care System State Concept, 2014–2020: Universal Health Care and Quality Management for Protection of Patient Rights	(i) Health in All Policies—a common state multisector approach, (ii) development of healthcare management, (iii) improvement of the system of financing the healthcare sector, (iv) development of quality healthcare services, (v) development of human resources in the healthcare sector, (vi) development of information systems for healthcare management, (vii) facilitation of maternal and child health, (viii) improvement of the prevention and management of priority communicable diseases, (ix) improvement of the prevention and monitoring of priority NCDs, and (x) development of the public system.

Country	Main National Health Sector Document(s)	Strategic Priorities
Kazakhstan	Program on healthcare development of the Republic of Kazakhstan for 2020–2025, approved by Government Decree N982 as of 26 December 2019	(i) Introduction of artificial intelligence and complete digitalization; (ii) mobile and web applications for informing and involving the population in protecting their own health; (iii) WHO Healthy Cities Initiative; (iv) increasing the level of literacy of the population on health issues and reducing behavioral risk factors; (v) development of personalized medicine; (vi) introduction of innovative treatment methods and technologies, including in the field of biopharmaceuticals; (vii) public–private partnership in healthcare; and (viii) increasing funding for healthcare.
Kyrgyz Republic	The Program of the Kyrgyz Republic Government on Public Health Protection and Health Care System Development for 2019–2030: "Healthy Person—Prosperous Country"	(i) Public health, (ii) development of the PHC, (iii) improving and rationalization of the hospital system, (iv) development of ambulance service, (v) laboratory services, (vi) drugs and medical devices, (vii) health care governance, (viii) human resources in healthcare, (ix) development of electronic health, (x) development of the financing system, and (xi) management of program implementation.
Mongolia	Mongolian State Policy on Health (approved in 2017). This policy is developed for 2017–2026 and indicated for regional and global cooperation for implementation of state health policy in eight key areas.	(i) Public health; (ii) medical care; (iii) human resources; (iv) health financing; (v) health technology; (vi) pharmaceuticals; (vii) IT and information management; and (viii) health sector management, organization, and transparency.
Pakistan	National Health Vision, 2016–2025	(i) Health financing, (ii) health service delivery, (iii) human resource for health, (iv) health information systems, (v) governance, (vi) essential medicines and technology, (vii) cross-sector linkages, and (viii) global health responsibilities.
Tajikistan	National Health Strategy of the Republic of Tajikistan, 2021–2030 (under development)	(i) Strengthening of mother, newborn, child, and adolescent health; (ii) prevention and control of infectious diseases; (iii) reducing the burden of noncommunicable and chronic diseases; (iv) health determinants and healthy lifestyle; (v) strengthening of public leadership for health protection; (vi) improving the quality and accessibility of prophylactic care; (vii) development of human resources; (viii) development of medical science and innovation; (ix) improving the drug supply and pharmaceutical activity; (x) modernization of production and technological base; and (xi) development of the financial base of health care.

Country	Main National Health Sector Document(s)	Strategic Priorities
Turkmenistan	National Health Strategy of Turkmenistan, 2021–2025 (government's health program)	(i) Creation of a unified healthcare prevention system; (ii) improving the population's immunization status; (iii) improving the immunization of the population against COVID-19; (iv) routine immunization; (v) strengthening the capacity of sanitary and epidemiological services and implementing cost-effective and quality programs; (vi) strengthening capacities of the PHC; (vii) further development of the pharmaceutical industry and ensuring good manufacturing practice; (viii) strengthening the health system; (ix) development of the digital medical system and electronic healthcare database; (x) strengthening of human resource capacities in the health sector; (xi) ensuring innovation research, research development, and reviewing of healthcare legislation; (xii) strengthening systems of data management and reporting; (xiii) strengthening national capacity on the core IHR areas of work; and (xiv) strengthening capacities in the health sector, related with the environment and health.
Uzbekistan	Healthcare system development concept of the Republic of Uzbekistan for 2019–2025	(i) Improving healthcare legislation; (ii) ensuring the integration of best management practices; (iii) improving the healthcare financing system, introducing a national state health insurance, and establishing a state health insurance fund; (iv) increasing the efficiency, quality, and availability of medical care with service delivery reforms and a focus on PHC, with NCDs as an entry point; (v) improvement of the protection system for mothers and children; (vi) development of private healthcare, public–private partnerships, and medical tourism; (vii) further development of the pharmaceutical industry and improvement of pricing mechanisms; (viii) formation of an effective system of training, retraining, and advanced training of medical personnel; (ix) widespread introduction of the e-health system; and (x) human health workforce reform.

IHR = International Health Regulations, IT = information technology, NCD = noncommunicable disease, PHC = primary health care, WHO = World Health Organization.
Source: ADB.

APPENDIX 3
SUMMARY OF CAREC COUNTRY POLICIES THAT REFLECT REGIONAL HEALTH COOPERATION

Country	Main Policy Document(s) Focusing on Regional/Global Health Cooperation (Laws, Decrees, Agreements, Polices, Plans)	Bilateral Agreements
Afghanistan	(1) National Health Policy 2019—crosscutting issues of regional health cooperation and integration (2) Regional Cooperation Component—increasing investment in health and addressing climate change in trans-Himalayan initiative (3) National Health Policy, 2015–2020 (IHR, Tobacco) (4) Tobacco Control Legislation 2014 (5) Afghan National Drug Action Plan, 2015–2019	(1) OIC (2) SAARC (3) CAREC (4) SCO (5) High-Level Expert Group on Drug Abuse (6) South Asia Co-operative Environment Programme (7) The International Centre for Integrated Mountain Development—on cooperation to mitigate the adverse effects of climate change across the trans-Himalayan region
Azerbaijan	(1) 'Azerbaijan 2020: Look into the Future' Concept of Development—defines strategic directions for international integration of the country in different sectors, including health. (2) Azerbaijan National Strategy for the Prevention and Control of Noncommunicable Diseases, 2015–2020 (Tobacco)	(1) BSEC (2) CIS (3) Cooperation Council of Turkic-Speaking States (Turkic Council) (4) OIC (5) Organization for Democracy and Economic Development (ODED-GUAM)
China, People's Republic of	(1) PRC Health Law (Law of PRC on Basic Medical and Health Care)—in effect since 1 June 2020 (2) International Health Regulation (IHR) of WHO—in effect since June 2007 (191 member countries)	(1) SCO (2) CPEC
Georgia	(1) Georgian Health Care System State Concept 2014–2020: Universal Health Care and Quality Management for Protection of Patient Rights (2) The EU–Georgia Association Agreement (3) Law of Georgia on Public Health (IHR) (4) Law of Georgia on Tobacco Control	(1) BSEC (2) ODED-GUAM

Country	Main Policy Document(s) Focusing on Regional/Global Health Cooperation (Laws, Decrees, Agreements, Polices, Plans)	Bilateral Agreements
Kazakhstan	(1) The law (code) on public health and the healthcare system of the Republic of Kazakhstan (adopted in 2009, last amended 7 July 2020) (2) Kazakhstan became a party to the WHO Framework Convention on Tobacco Control on 22 April 2007	(1) CIS (2) Cooperation Council of Turkic-Speaking States (Turkic Council) (3) Eurasian Economic Union (EAEU) (4) OIC (5) ABEC (6) Bilateral agreements (TB/HIV) with the Kyrgyz Republic and Tajikistan (no progress made yet) (7) SCO
Kyrgyz Republic	(1) The Program of the Kyrgyz Republic Government on Public Health Protection and Health Care System Development for 2019–2030: 'Healthy Person—Prosperous Country'; establishment of the national network of 'healthy cities,' with integration into the international network and attraction of additional investments for the development of cities; development and implementation of e-health synchronization mechanisms with international standards and integration processes (EAEU, SCO). (2) The Program of the Kyrgyz Republic Government on Public Health Protection and Health Care System Development for 2019–2030: 'Healthy Person—Prosperous Country' (IHR, harmonization of transborder policy within the IHR)	(1) CIS (2) Cooperation Council of Turkic-Speaking States (Turkic Council) (3) EAEU (4) OIC (5) ABEC (6) Bilateral agreements (TB/HIV) with Kazakhstan and Tajikistan (no progress made yet) (7) SCO
Mongolia	(1) The Law on Health (1998, amended several times from 2002 to 2016): The roles and duties of local government to collaborate with international organizations for the implementation of health programs (2) The Law on Medicines and Medical Devices (approved in 2010): Regional cooperation for importing and exporting medicines and medical devices and bioactive products (3) The Law on COVID (approved in 2020): Cooperation with bordering countries on regulating the restrictions of movement of passengers and vehicles across borders (4) Mongolian Sustainable Development Vision for 2030 (approved by Parliament in 2016) (5) Mongolian State Policy on Health, 2017–2026: Regional and global cooperation for the implementation of state health policy in eight key areas, namely (a) public health; (b) medical care; (c) human resources; (d) health financing; (e) health technology; (f) pharmaceuticals; (g) IT and information management; and (h) health sector management, organization, and transparency.	(1) Mongolia is a member of the CAREC program and has been actively engaging in regional economic and social cooperation. (2) Mongolia joined the Asia-Europe Meeting during its summit in Helsinki in 2006. (3) Mongolia joined the Organization for Security and Cooperation in Europe in 2012. (4) Mongolia became a member of the Food and Agriculture Organization in 1973. (5) Mongolia has participated in the Ulaanbaatar Dialogue on Northeast Asian Security initiative since 2013.

Country	Main Policy Document(s) Focusing on Regional/ Global Health Cooperation (Laws, Decrees, Agreements, Polices, Plans)	Bilateral Agreements
	(6) Mongolian foreign policy concept: Improve education, health, and social protection services in line with international standards and requirements and facilitate the study and implementation of the experience of countries that have made progress in this area (7) UN Convention Against Illicit Traffic in Narcotic Drugs and Psychotropic Substances (8) WHO FCTC	
Pakistan	(1) Bill to establish a National Food Safety, Animal and Plant Safety Regulatory Authority, specifying functions and powers of the authority, such as coordinating with international organizations, representing Pakistani interests at international forums, and entering into arrangements and agreements relating to bilateral and multilateral cooperation with regard to SPS matters. (2) Pakistan became party to WHO FCTC in 2005. (3) The Pakistan Polio Eradication Programme is a public–private partnership led by the Government of Pakistan and spearheaded by partners such as WHO, UNICEF, BMGF, Rotary International, and CDC.	(1) OIC (2) China–Pakistan Economic Corridor (CPEC) (3) Economic Cooperation Organization (4) SAARC
Tajikistan	(1) Health Care Code of the Republic of Tajikistan (adopted in 2017): Provides a general regulatory framework for international cooperation in the field of public health with international organizations and relevant bodies of foreign states. More focused regulatory base in the respective technical areas are provided in the following laws: "On Ensuring Biological Safety and Biological Protection" (2021); "On Veterinary Medicine" (2016); "On Food Safety" (2012); "On Quarantine and Plant Protection" (2019); "On Biological Management and Production" (2013); "On the Protection of Population and Territories from Natural and Technogenic Emergencies" (2004) (2) Labor Code (No. 1329 of 23 July 2016) (3) National Health Strategy of the Republic of Tajikistan, 2021–2030: Has a section on international cooperation in health (focus on Shanghai Cooperation Organization and CIS) (4) Law of the Republic of Tajikistan: "On Ensuring Biological Safety and Biological Protection," adopted 29 January 2021, No. 1759 (IHR) (5) Law of the Republic of Tajikistan (No. 1484 of 2 January 2018) "On Limiting the Use of Tobacco Products"	(1) OIC (2) SCO (3) Bilateral agreements (TBs/HIV) with Kazakhstan and the Kyrgyz Republic (no progress made yet) (4) Collective Security Treaty Organization (https://odkb-csto.org/ countries/tadzhikistan/) (5) CIS

Country	Main Policy Document(s) Focusing on Regional/ Global Health Cooperation (Laws, Decrees, Agreements, Polices, Plans)	Bilateral Agreements
Turkmenistan	1) National Health Strategy of Turkmenistan, 2021–2025: Focus on international cooperation in education and training of health professionals 2) Newly updated (17.04.2021) Acute Infectious Disease Preparedness and Response Plan of Turkmenistan (CPRP): Focus on organizing international coordination, cooperation, and emergency assistance 3) The national program 2021–2025 for strengthening the capacity of the population to fight infectious disease 4) National Plan for Immunization and Distribution of COVID-19 Vaccines in Turkmenistan 5) Law of Turkmenistan "On Protecting the Health of Citizens from the Effects of Tobacco Smoke and the Consequences of Tobacco Product Consumption" 7) National program on the implementation of the WHO Framework Convention on Tobacco Control in 2017: The new tobacco control strategy and action plan for 2022–2025 is being developed. 8) National NCD strategy and action plan for 2021–2025 RMNCAH strategy and action plan for 2021–2025: Law to Protect Citizen Health National Strategy on Healthy Nutrition National Strategy and Action Plan on Mental Health for 2018–2022 National Strategy for Increasing Physical Activity Among the Population for 2018–2024 National Strategy and Action Plan on Alcohol for 2018–2024 National Plan for Pandemic Influenza Preparedness in Turkmenistan (2019) Strategic Plan on Strengthening Control Measures for Viral Hepatitis in Turkmenistan, 2019–2030	1) OIC 2) CIS 3) Cooperation Council of Turkic-Speaking States (Turkic Council) 4) Gas pipeline Turkmenistan–Afghanistan–Pakistan–India 5) SCO 6) Intergovernmental Turkmen-Kyrgyz Commission for trade-economic, scientific-technical, and humanitarian cooperation 7) Turkmen–Qatari Commission on trade-economic cooperation 8) Intergovernmental Agreement on the Implementation of the International Transit-Transport Route Caspian Sea–Black Sea 9) International Monetary Fund, the World Bank, European Bank for Reconstruction and Development, ADB, Islamic Development Bank, and others. 10) Turkmenistan–Uzbekistan–Kazakhstan–PRC gas pipeline 11) Memorandum of understanding was signed between the 'Turkmennebit' State Concern and the ARETI International Group of Companies 12) CAREC Corridor 2 and Corridor 3 13) Provision of procurement services between Turkmenistan and UNICEF
Uzbekistan	1) The Welfare Improvement Strategy of the Republic of Uzbekistan for 2013–2015 plans to increase cooperation with international organizations in various sectors, including the development of human capital and the social sector. 2) National Programme on Tobacco Control, 2011–2020 3) National and Central Asian Republics TB control, strategy 4) National and Central Asian Republics immunization strategy	1) OIC 2) CIS 3) Cooperation Council of Turkic-Speaking States (Turkic Council) 4) Eurasian Economic Union (EAEU) 5) Shanghai Cooperation Organization (SCO) 6) International financial funds: World Bank, ADB, EBRD, IBRD

ADB = Asian Development Bank; ABEC = Almaty–Bishkek Economic Corridor; BMGF = Bill & Melinda Gates Foundation; BSEC = Black Sea Economic Cooperation; CAREC = Central Asia Regional Economic Cooperation Program; CDC = Centers for Disease Control and Prevention; CIS = Commonwealth of Independent States; CPEC = China–Pakistan Economic Corridor; COVID 19 = coronavirus disease; EAEU = Eurasian Economic Union; EBRD = European Bank of Reconstruction and Development; EU = European Union; FCTC = Framework Convention on Tobacco Control; IBRD = International Bank for Reconstruction and Development; IHR = International Health Regulations; IT = information technology; NCD = noncommunicable disease; ODED-GUAM = Organization for Democracy and Economic Development—Georgia, Ukraine, Azerbaijan, and Moldova; OIC = Organisation of Islamic Cooperation; RMNCAH = reproductive maternal, newborn, child and adolescent health; SAARC = South Asian Association for Regional Cooperation; SCO = Shanghai Cooperation Organization; TB = tuberculosis; UNICEF = United Nations Children's Fund; WHO = World Health Organization.

Source: ADB.

APPENDIX 4

SUMMARY OF CAREC COUNTRIES' INSTITUTIONAL ARRANGEMENTS FOR REGIONAL COOPERATION

Country	Main National Institution Responsible for Regional Cooperation in Health	Main Function(s) for Guiding and Implementing Regional Cooperation in Health
Afghanistan	(1) Ministry of Public Health, Deputy Minister for Policy and Planning, Technical Advisory Group (2) Health Committee of the Parliament (3) President (4) Ministry of Foreign Affairs, Regional Cooperation Directorate	Review the technical RHC policy, strategies, regulations, and laws prepared by technical health departments. Review and provide feedback; the general Parliament meeting ratifies the relevant policies and laws. Communicate and inform the partners in regional cooperation about the laws. Develop and implement projects in the areas of RHC and/or GHC; ensure the respective budget planning (in partnership with the Ministry of Finance and Ministry of Economy). Organize and guide international exchanges and cooperation, international publicity, and foreign aid in the health sector.
Azerbaijan	(1) Parliament (2) Department of International Relations, Ministry of Health (3) Agency for Mandatory Medical Insurance (4) Food Safety Agency of the Republic of Azerbaijan	
China, People's Republic of	(1) Department of International Cooperation, National Health Commission (2) Department of International Economic and Financial Cooperation, Ministry of Finance	

Country	Main National Institution Responsible for Regional Cooperation in Health	Main Function(s) for Guiding and Implementing Regional Cooperation in Health
Georgia	(1) Ministry of Internally Displaced Persons from Occupied Territories; Labor, Health and Social Affairs; Department of Policy; and International Relations Unit (2) LEPL-the National Centre for Disease Control and Public Health (NCDC): almost all departments collaborate with international partners (except for the administrative department) (3) LEPL-the State Regulation Agency for Medical Activities (4) LEPL-the Emergency Situations Coordination and Urgent Assistance Centre (5) LEPL-the National Health Agency: implementing state healthcare programs (7) National Food Agency, Ministry of Environmental Protection and Agriculture (8) Health Care and Social Issues Committee of the Parliament of Georgia	
Kazakhstan	(1) National Coordination Council on Health Care Protection (2) Department of International Cooperation and Integration, Ministry of Health (3) Sanitary and Epidemiological Control Committee, Ministry of Health of the Republic of Kazakhstan (4) Ministry of Agriculture, Veterinary Supervision and Control Committee	
Kyrgyz Republic	Ministry of Health of the Kyrgyz Republic	
Mongolia	(1) Parliament of Mongolia (2) Government of Mongolia (Ministry of Health, Ministry of Foreign Affairs, and Ministry of Finance) (3) Provincial and city governments (4) Provincial and district health departments	
Pakistan	(1) Parliamentary Standing Committees on Health (2) Ministry of National Health Services, Regulation and Coordination (3) Ministry of Planning, Development and Reforms	
Tajikistan	(1) Government of the Republic of Tajikistan and Parliament (2) Ministry of Health and Social Protection of Population of the Republic of Tajikistan and their states (sanitary epidemiological control, farm control, and accreditation) (3) Ministry of Agriculture and Environmental Protection (4) Ministry of Foreign Affairs of the Republic of Tajikistan (5) Ministry of Justice of the Republic of Tajikistan	

Country	Main National Institution Responsible for Regional Cooperation in Health	Main Function(s) for Guiding and Implementing Regional Cooperation in Health
Turkmenistan	1) Government of Turkmenistan, Ministry of Health and Medical Industry 2) Ministry of Finance and Economy 3) Ministry of Foreign Affairs of Turkmenistan 4) Other involved ministries and agencies	
Uzbekistan	1) Parliament of the Republic of Uzbekistan 2) Government of the Republic of Uzbekistan (Ministry of Health, Ministry of Foreign Affairs, and Ministry of Finance) 3) Provincial and city governments 4) Provincial and district health departments	

RHC = regional health cooperation, GHC = Global Health Cooperation, LEPL = Legal Entity under Public Law.
Source: ADB.

APPENDIX 5
SUMMARY OF LESSONS LEARNED DURING THE PANDEMIC

Many lessons have been learned during the COVID-19 pandemic that underscore the importance of factors influencing health sector resilience and health security. Among these factors are responsiveness and preparedness for public health threats and the ability to act promptly and have sufficient funds and technical and human capacity for emergency situations. Continuous investments in social determinants of health, considering gender issues, the needs of the vulnerable, and latest innovations, have also proven to be of major importance for the stability of a health system. Key lessons are listed in Table A5.

Table A5: Summary of Lessons Learned on COVID-19 Response

Lesson	Details
Clear governance structures and coordination mechanisms	Trust in government competence has proven to be key for public acceptance of strong government mandates. Transparent decision-making processes are important to build trust and acceptance among the public.
Effective communication and public trust	Transparent decision-making processes to build trust and acceptance among the public were important. The validity of the background and scientific basis to decisions and restrictions, supported by technical bodies and data, has proven vital to achieve population compliance and commitment. Lessons learned also show the importance of political leaders providing role model examples, for instance, when government officials observe physical distancing.
Mitigation response speed	Countries that acted quickly and comprehensively fared better than those who delayed responses.[a] Mitigation policies, including closure of nonessential businesses, restrictions on gatherings and movement, and stay-at-home orders, have been critical to controlling the COVID-19 pandemic in many countries.[b] Countries with ability to monitor interventions have been able to delay the propagation of the COVID-19 spread, thus, buying valuable time and avoiding the collapse of healthcare services.
Rapid release of financing	COVID-19 revealed that rapid response funding was important for countries to take quick action in a structured manner.
Sufficient surge capacity	Sufficient, well-trained, and efficiently distributed workforce to manage case surges; well-equipped primary care facilities; well-equipped hospitals (adequate bed capacity, sufficient and well-equipped ICUs, and proper diagnostic capacity); satisfactory PPE and adequate laboratory systems and testing capacity; and surveillance and health information systems.
Leveraging innovations	Driving innovation, even during times of crisis, was critical to support response. The COVID-19 pandemic has highlighted how innovative solutions can contribute to solving a health crisis. Since early 2020, numerous governments, organizations, companies, and academic institutions have rapidly developed innovative solutions for managing the COVID-19 crisis.

Lesson	Details
Need for psychosocial support	During the many lockdowns, the low quality of housing in many countries harshly affected the mental health of people, especially among the most vulnerable segments of the population. Investments in education, including distance learning, are important to keep up the level of knowledge and pace of learning children have prior to a health crisis. Government support to businesses and psychosocial support for health workers and the general public (e.g., hotlines) are needed.
Need for gender equity	Gender inequality increases in health crisis situations.[c] The COVID-19 pandemic showed that women could not access health services as frequently as prior to the crisis. Decreased working hours resulted in decreased earnings for many women. Because of that, women were facing difficulties in affording basic expenses such as utilities and rent. Besides that, domestic violence occurred more frequently.[d] The overall burden affected the mental and emotional health of women.
Sufficient access to services and financial protection	Countries with policies that are closely aligned with UHC frameworks and global health security have generally fared better and might be better equipped to recover after COVID-19 compared with countries with health systems that are not aligned to either framework.[e]
Investing in social determinants of health	Investments in UHC are not only important to strengthen health system resilience, but they are also crucial for improving social determinants of health to protect the poor and vulnerable.

COVID-19 = coronavirus disease, ICU = intensive care unit, PPE = personal protective equioment, UHC = universal health coverage.

[a] The Independent Panel for Pandemic Preparedness and Response. 20 21. *COVID-19: Make it the Last Pandemic.* https://theindependentpanel.org/wp-content/uploads/2021/05/COVID-19-Make-it-the-Last-Pandemic_final.pdf

[b] J.A. Fuller et al., CDC COVID-19 Response Team. 2021. Mitigation Policies and COVID-19-Associated Mortality—37 European Countries. 23 January 2020–30 June 2020. *MMWR Morbidity Mortality Weekly Report.* 70 (2). pp. 58–62.

[c] T. Khitarishvili. 2016. Gender Dimensions of Inequality in the Countries of Central Asia, South Caucasus, and Western CIS. *Working Paper Series. No. 858.* New York: Levy Economics Institute of Bard College; United Nations Children's Fund (UNICEF). 2016. *Rapid Review on Inclusion and Gender Equality in Central and Eastern Europe, the Caucasus and Central Asia.* Geneva; OECD. 2019. *Promoting Gender Equality in Eurasia. Better Policies for Women's Economic Empowerment. Draft Background* Note. Paris.

[d] UN Women. 2020. *The Impact of COVID-19 on Women's and Men's Lives and Livelihoods in Europe and Central Asia: Preliminary Results from a Rapid Gender Assessment.* Istanbul.

[e] A. Lal et al. 2021. Fragmented Health Systems in COVID-19: Rectifying the Misalignment between Global Health Security and Universal Health Coverage. *Lancet.* 397 (10268). pp. 61–67.